Hawker Typhoon

The RAF's Ground-Breaking Fighter-Bomber

TONY BUTTLER

HISTORIC MILITARY AIRCRAFT SERIES, VOLUME 5

Front cover image: Manufacturer's photo of what appears to be Typhoon Mk IB EK266, probably taken prior to delivery since no squadron markings have been applied. (Hawker Aircraft)

Back cover image: Hawker Typhoons of 56 Squadron with their 'US' codes formate for the official cameraman on 21 April 1943. This was one of the first Typhoon photos to be revealed to the public, just a few days later. (Peter Green)

Title page image: Typhoon R8809 photographed on 15 May 1943 while the aircraft was in the hands of A&AEE Boscombe Down. It features a sliding hood and the pilot appears not to be wearing a flying helmet. (Phil Butler)

Contents page image: Typhoon Mk IB JR128 with a bubble canopy was used by Hawker Aircraft to produce a series of publicity pictures. The aircraft carries the code 'HF-L' for 183 Squadron. (Hawker Aircraft)

Published by Key Books
An imprint of Key Publishing Ltd
PO Box 100
Stamford
Lincs PE19 1XQ

www.keypublishing.com

Acknowledgements
The author wishes to thank the following for their contributions to this book:

Phil Butler; Chris Farara; Trevor Brockington and Roy Gasson (Napier Power Heritage Trust); Martin Derry; Peter Green; Tim Kershaw (Jet Age Museum); and the staff of the National Archives at Kew. Special thanks must go to Chris Thomas, to former pilot Derek Tapson and also to the Key Publishing team.

Uncredited images are from the author's collection. While every effort has been made to contact copyright holders, we apologise for any errors or omissions.

The right of Tony Buttler to be identified as the author of this book has been asserted in accordance with the Copyright, Designs and Patents Act 1988 Sections 77 and 78.

Copyright © Tony Buttler, 2021

ISBN 978 1 913870 90 4

Typeset by SJmagic DESIGN SERVICES, India.

Contents

Introduction

A lthough first designed as a fighter, the Hawker Typhoon – the 'Tiffie' or 'Tiffy' – achieved a tremendous reputation as a ground-attack aircraft and tank buster through its ability to hit Axis ground forces so hard during the fighting in Europe in 1944/45. This was quite remarkable since the path the Typhoon had to follow to achieve success proved to be long and difficult. There were troubles with its Napier Sabre engine (engine problems brought the end of the concurrent Hawker Tornado fitted with a Rolls-Royce Vulture) and failures of the airframe. Once these 'teething troubles' had at least been brought under control, the Typhoon's time 'at the top' was then relatively short because it was retired soon after the end of the war to be replaced by more advanced types such as the follow-on Hawker Tempest.

But it took its chance! After achieving some success as a true fighter, the need for a new ground-attack fighter-bomber to succeed the tank-busting versions of the company's Hurricane meant that the perfect role was waiting for the Typhoon. During the last year of World War Two, following the D-Day landings in June 1944, the type went on to perform a critical role in the European theatre. In addition to having little in the way of a post-war life the Typhoon also never operated outside Western Europe, so to leave such a record of success over such a short time period is nothing short of outstanding! If in some respects the Typhoon was not a world-beater, it was the perfect aircraft for the job that was required of it.

Most volumes documenting the Typhoon usually cover it in conjunction with the Tempest, so perhaps it is now time to give Hawker's heavyweight a volume of its own, because the Typhoon won true fame as a quite formidable fighter-bomber.

Tony Buttler
Bretforton, February 2021

Chapter 1

Development Process

The Hawker Hurricane fighter is, simply through its involvement in the Battle of Britain, one of the most well-known of all aeroplanes. However, after that critical battle developments in enemy fighters soon left the Hurricane behind, although later versions were configured for ground attack and armed with cannon and/or bombs. As such this extended the type's operational career and at the same time confirmed the immense value of a new category of aircraft – the fighter-bomber. Hawker followed the Hurricane with the Typhoon and the unsuccessful Tornado and, although the

Typhoon Mk 1B JR128 was photographed in May 1944 having just completed a modification programme at Hawker Aircraft. It still wears code letters 'HF-L', the markings of its previous owner, 183 Squadron. (Hawker Aircraft)

Prior to the arrival of the Typhoon in the role, the responsibility for the RAF's ground-attack and 'tank-busting' duties had fallen to a large extent on the shoulders of the older Hurricane. This picture shows a bomb-carrying Hurricane Mk IIB BE485 in 1941. (Hawker Aircraft)

former entered service as a fighter, its performance proved limited when flying at altitude. However, the Typhoon's heavy structure and four wing-mounted cannon provided an ideal basis for development as the next fighter-bomber.

Hawker 'N' and 'R'

Specification F.18/37 of March 1938 requested a new high-speed single-seat fighter to replace the Spitfire and Hurricane (which of course at the time had hardly begun their own careers). The new type would be armed with twelve 0.303in Browning machine guns and have a top speed of at least 400mph (644kph) at 15,000ft with a service ceiling of at least 35,000ft. Design proposals came from Bristol, Gloster, Hawker and Supermarine and the winning selections were two versions of the same aircraft from Hawker, one powered by a single Napier Sabre engine and the second by a Rolls-Royce Vulture. Design work on Hawker's new Sabre-powered fighter project had started on 5 April 1937, the layout at this stage providing a wing-span of 40ft (12m). On 19 June Hawker opened discussions with the National Physical Laboratory about potential problems with the airscrew and compressibility effects at high speeds (the effect of the compressibility of air becomes more prominent, and has a greater effect on aerodynamic performance, at high speeds), so even at this early stage the potential for reaching a very high airspeed was there along with the problems that this would bring.

The firm called its two fighters the 'N' type (for Napier Sabre) and 'R' type (Rolls-Royce Vulture), the original Hawker diaries confirming the use of the letters 'N' and 'R'. In April 1938 construction began on an 'R' type mock-up and in mid-April models of both 'N' and 'R' types were sent to the Royal Aircraft Establishment (RAE) for wind-tunnel testing. The official tender in response to F.18/37 was sent to the Air Ministry on 30 April. On 30 August 1938 Hawker learnt that it had won the competition and that two examples of each type were to be ordered (all four were covered by Contract B.815124/38 of December 1938). The Mock-Up Conference for both versions was held at Kingston on 16 December, and on 10 July 1939 the Air Ministry ordered 1,000 production fighters – 500 of each type – and issued instructions to Hawker to begin tooling up.

Model of one of the Supermarine proposals for F.18/37, the Type 327 which had six 20mm cannon mounted in the wing roots. (Joe Cherrie)

The Sabre and Vulture liquid-cooled piston engines were both intended to provide at least 2,000hp (1,490kW), the planning for these motors having started in 1937. However, Napier first began to look into the development of a 2,000hp (1,490kW) twin-crankshaft-type engine as early as late 1935, at a time when the most-powerful engines then available fell within in the 1,000–1,200hp (746–895kW) class. Napier continued to concentrate on an 'H' type of cylinder arrangement for the follow-on to its earlier H-24-configuration Dagger aero engine. The firm's previous engines were of the vertical H-type and were air-cooled but the Sabre cylinders were arranged horizontally and the engine was to be liquid-cooled; the older types' poppet valves were also superseded by sleeve valves. The H-configuration offered a compact layout formed by two horizontally opposed engines lying one atop (horizontal) or beside (vertical) the other with the result that because the cylinders were opposed, the motion in one cylinder bank was balanced by the motion on the opposing side. Therefore, it was expected that there should be little or no vibration.

Sydney Camm, master aircraft designer at Hawker, who was responsible for the Typhoon and many of the fighter types that followed. (Hawker Aircraft)

The resulting Sabre was a huge 24-cylinder sleeve-valve unit with the cylinders arranged in four banks of six, the pistons driving two crankshafts. The first examples were ready for testing in January 1938, although at that stage power was limited to 1,350hp (1,007kW), but early production models were capable of 2,200hp (1,640kW) and in late-model prototypes the output rose to 3,500hp (2,610kW). The Sabre's first mount was the Napier-Heston Racer, an aircraft designed purely for

January 1944 photo print showing a Napier Sabre II engine. (Napier)

Rolls-Royce Vulture engine. The print is dated June 1942. (Rolls-Royce)

capturing speed records but which in the end flew just once, in June 1940. The new engine passed its Air Ministry 100 hours type test in June 1940.

Many observers felt that it was an incautious policy to embark on such an advanced design and in the end the Sabre experienced a long and very difficult development, but once it had matured it proved to be an excellent power unit and became one of the world's most powerful in-line piston aircraft engines. When the Typhoon was designed, however, the Sabre was still somewhat of a speculative proposition which, although offering great promise, was far from being thoroughly developed and tested. The development problems became such that during 1940 the Air Staff considered fitting an American Wright Cyclone engine (used in the B-17, among other US-built aircraft) to the Typhoon. Drawings were also produced for a Duplex Cyclone (which went on to be used in aircraft including the B-29) installation in the Tornado and an engine was apparently delivered to Hawker in October. However, it was never fitted to an airframe and all work on this idea was suspended officially in July 1941.

In contrast, Rolls-Royce effectively took two of its V-12 Peregrine engines and joined them together (one atop the other with upright and inverted 'V's) using a new crankcase to produce the 'X-24' Vulture. With the Rolls-Royce solution all four cylinder banks drove a single centrally mounted crankshaft. At the start the Vulture offered some promise and was designed to produce around 1,750hp (1,305kW), but problems meant that in service the engines had to be de-rated to 1,450–1,550hp (1,080–1,156kW).

Since the Napier and Rolls-Royce units required different engine mountings, it was never possible to make them interchangeable, but having them both meant that one could act as an insurance against failure of the other, which was what eventually happened. Although essentially the same aircraft, the Typhoon and Tornado's powerplants also required different cooling systems and other associated items, but the two airframes would have common centre fuselages, rear monocoques, tail units and wings.

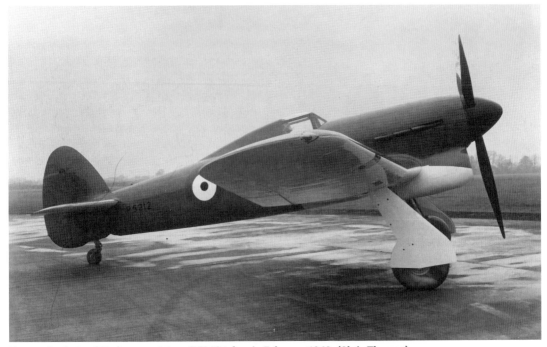

Very early photo of Typhoon prototype P5212 taken in February 1940. (Chris Thomas)

Typhoon prototype P5216, at this stage armed with twelve machine guns housed just outboard of the undercarriage, at A&AEE Boscombe Down in October 1940. Neither the hinged wheel doors nor the windows in the canopy fairing were adopted for production. (Peter Green)

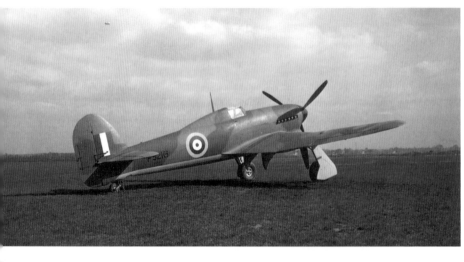

In due course P5216 was rearmed with four cannon as shown here, but with only part of each barrel inside a fairing. (Crown Copyright)

In August 1939 the Vulture-powered 'R' type was named Tornado and in December, the 'N' became the Typhoon (the two differed sufficiently that they could not share the same name with different mark numbers). The first batch of Tornados was to be constructed at Hawker's Kingston factory while the Typhoons were to be assembled by Gloster Aircraft at Hucclecote; a decision to make four-cannon wings at Gloster and 12-gun wings at Kingston was confirmed in March 1940. The decision to switch the entire Tornado production programme to Avro was made on 23 October 1940 and was taken because that company (a sister firm within the Hawker Siddeley Group) by that time had experience with the Vulture engine on its Manchester bomber.

The first Tornado prototype P5219 pictured in October 1939 with the radiator in its original position beneath the fuselage, level with the wing. With the metal canopy fairing, the lack of vision to the rear for the pilot can be imagined. (Peter Green)

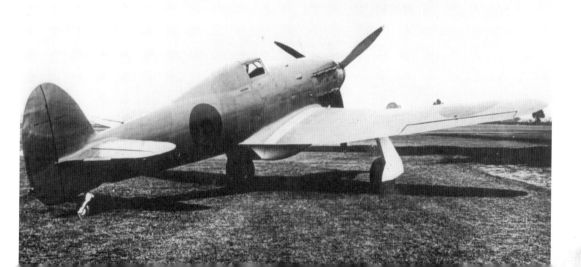

P5219 again, now with the radiator moved to the chin position. Note the twin rows of exhaust stubs. (Crown Copyright)

Mounting the radiator beneath the Sabre-powered Typhoon's nose gave the aircraft a very aggressive appearance, while at this stage the Tornado's radiator was positioned underneath the middle fuselage and level with the wing. Forecasts made in August 1940 had indicated a top speed for the Typhoon of 400mph (644kph) at 15,500ft with a slightly lower figure, 380mph (612kph) at 17,500ft, for the Tornado fitted with a Vulture II.

Large-scale production of the Tornado and the Typhoon was well advanced when in May 1940 Germany invaded France. This emergency prompted the Air Ministry, at Whitsun, to remove the priority allocated to Typhoon and Tornado orders to enable Hurricane output to be accelerated in readiness for expected attacks on the British mainland. In light of the role played by the Hurricane in the Battle of Britain this decision was very wise, but the move seriously delayed the ordering of materials and any sub-contract arrangements for its replacement. On 12 June 1940, Hawker designer Sydney Camm wrote to N E Rowe, Director of Technical Development (DTD) at the Ministry of Aircraft Production (MAP), asking that the work should resume immediately. By October the Typhoon and Tornado had been restored to the future programme and on 6 October the Air Staff stated a requirement for the production of both types fitted with four 20mm cannon as early as possible.

The first prototype Typhoon had 12 0.303in Browning machine guns but in due course the second flew with four cannon. The machine guns were placed six in each wing in groups of three and on a cradle which was easily detached from the aircraft's structure. The first layout with wing-mounted cannon was apparently proposed in August 1938 and Camm presented a rough scheme to fit two Hispano cannon in each wing to AVM Sholto Douglas, Assistant Chief of the Air Staff (ACAS) on 23 December 1940. Douglas considered it essential to continue with the first two prototypes without alterations (ie, with 0.303in machine guns) but added that, in view of some ongoing experimental work in connection with the effect of gunfire on armour protected aeroplanes: 'We should look into the problem of providing the Hispano installation in the wings of the third and fourth prototype aeroplanes'. The thick wings on the new design would prove ideal for taking the bigger weapons.

On 11 April 1940 it was decided to proceed with a trial installation of six guns in the Tornado. By April 1941 the Air Staff viewed the installation of six 20mm cannon as an urgent operational development, and on 2 July Hawker was contracted to produce one set of 'Universal Wings' for the Typhoon capable of taking six cannon, two cannon and eight Browning machine guns, or 12 Brownings. Later, six 0.5in machine guns were added to the options, but in the end the four-cannon

Comparative front views of Typhoon prototype P5216 (above) and Tornado P5219 (below) after the latter's radiator had been moved. Apart from the single rows of exhaust stubs and the cannon on the Typhoon, the main difference was that the wings on the Tornado were mounted lower on the fuselage than on the Typhoon. (Crown Copyright)

Excellent side view of the second Tornado prototype P5224. This picture was taken in March 1941. (Peter Green)

P5224 again, this time in October 1941 and showing its flaps in the lowered position. (Peter Green)

This picture of production Typhoon EK497 highlights the different appearances of the prototypes and production machines with their rocket launch rails and the general wear of constant flying. This example still has the car-door cockpit and a three-blade propeller and shows no unit markings since it was an A&AEE trials aircraft, undertaking much of the initial and development testing of rocket projectiles on the Typhoon. (Peter Green)

arrangement would become standard (the six-cannon fitting was dropped since this required the drilling of the metal structure which could reduce the overall strength of the wing).

Avro's Tornado production run was covered by Contract 121248/39, but only aircraft serial numbers R7936 to R7938 were produced (and just the first of these flew) before the order was cancelled. In April 1941 the decision was made to install Vulture V engines in all Tornados from the start of production, but in July all flying with this engine was suspended owing to connecting-rod-bolt fractures. The first Vulture V suffered from persistent connecting-rod fractures, which badly affected the Manchester, so on 15 October all Vulture development work was stopped. The Tornado development and production programme came to a halt that same day, but by then (on 21 April 1941) the Sabre II version of Napier's engine had been introduced to the production line.

Dead Ends

In 1941, there were plans to take the Typhoon to sea, an idea prompted by delays with the contemporary Blackburn Firebrand naval fighter. However, it was soon clear that the Hawker P.1009 'Sea Typhoon' would require a substantial redesign from the land-based version, making it virtually a new aircraft. Eventually, RAF reports noted how the Typhoon was a good 'bomber destroyer' but lacked the manoeuvrability needed for combat, when the Navy's requirement was actually two-fold, for an 'Umbrella Fighter' and a long-distance escort fighter (the Service was trying to merge the two). The project was soon abandoned and the Navy went on to acquire the navalised version of the Supermarine Spitfire, which it called the Seafire.

The Typhoon's moves from fighter to fighter-bomber and to reconnaissance are covered elsewhere, but it was also considered as a night-fighter. In June 1942 one Typhoon, serial R7651, was sent to Ford to join the Fighter Interception Unit (FIU), where it was found that the type was easier to fly on instruments than either the Spitfire or the Hurricane. Thus it seemed quite possible that Hawker's aircraft, with a new sliding canopy and better cockpit lighting, could make a good night fighter.

On 20 July the Air Staff decided to take this a step further. Serial R7630 was selected to begin trials with a Douglas Boston that was kitted out with what was known as Turbinlite – the installation of air-interception (AI) radar plus a massive searchlight in the nose. Having spotted a target the Boston would illuminate it with the searchlight, thereby giving the Typhoon the opportunity to shoot the

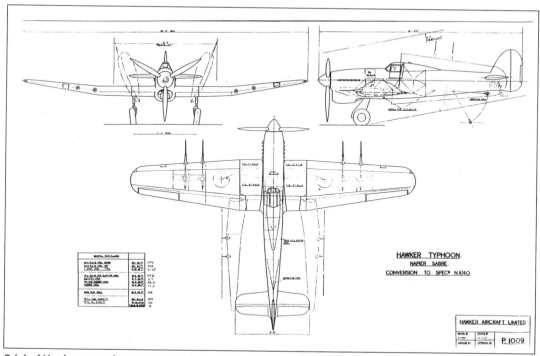

Original Hawker general arrangement drawing of the P.1009 project, the proposed Navy Typhoon. The aircraft had a span of 50ft (15.24m), length 35ft 8.5in (10.88m) and wing area 354sq ft (32.92sq m). The four cannon are spread well out along the wings. (Hawker)

Above left and above right: **The Typhoon night-fighter prototype was R7881 converted from a standard production machine. The view on the left (courtesy of Hawker) shows the aircraft in its original form, while on the right R7881 is seen later in its night-fighter career after having acquired a four-blade propeller. Note the radar aerials protruding on the wings. Long-range tanks were carried permanently, because the radar equipment filled the normal wing-tank space.**

enemy aircraft down. A problem here was that the Typhoon's minimum speed was not that much higher than the Boston's cruising speed, which made formation flight at night quite problematic. However, fitted with its own AI radar, it was clear that the Typhoon offered considerable potential as a night-fighter.

As a result Hawker fitted an AI Mk VI radar transmitter and receiver in R7881's port wing with a small display in the cockpit. The radar replaced the port main fuel tank, the lost capacity being replaced by permanent 45 gal (205l) tanks under each wing. The assessment of this radar installation was undertaken by RAE Farnborough in April 1943, after which the FIU began what proved to be a successful trials programme. R7881 went on to make several uneventful night-time patrols over London during November 1943 and gave a good account of itself with its radar, which provided coverage at target ranges of between 500ft minimum and 9,000ft maximum; in addition the Typhoon's speed and manoeuvrability permitted it to make quick intercepts against trial targets.

This much better quality photo shows R7881 as first converted to night-fighter configuration with its new camouflage scheme. (Hawker)

Two views of R8694 with the experimental annular radiator installed for its Sabre IV engine and a four-blade propeller.

However, the night-fighter Typhoon would never enter service, in part because the de Havilland Mosquito night-fighter was even better. R7881, the sole example converted to this standard and designated NF Mk IB, had its radar removed and in July 1944 was retired to No. 3 Tactical Exercise Unit at Honiley.

In 1942/43 Typhoon R8694 was used by Napier for trials to assess the effects of fitting an annular radiator with a Sabre IV engine. The annular radiator replaced the familiar underslung type, the new cowling being formed along the lines used in radial engine design with a fan incorporated in the airscrew spinner, which then forced the cooling air through the radiator mounted immediately at the rear (ie, fan-assisted cooling). It is understood that very successful flights were made by R8694 with this neat arrangement and an increase in performance was recorded (some sources indicate a maximum level speed of 452mph/727kph).

During its time with Napier (from September 1942) R8694 flew trials with Sabre IV and Sabre VI engines, with and without the annular radiator, and the programme was continued using Tempest serial NV768, which then flew with several different types of annular radiator and hollow spinner. However, although the annular radiator with its engine-driven fan and axially sliding exit gill had originally been designed to make the Sabre V suitable for tropical operations, the trials with R8694 eventually established that the extra weight and the complication of the fan were not justified on a fighter, and were unnecessary for operation in temperate climates.

Nose view of an unidentified Typhoon Mk IB taken in April 1943.

Chapter 2

The Tornado

Flight Testing

With two different sets of prototypes for Tornado and Typhoon there were of course two separate flight-test programmes. This chapter looks at the former and also takes the Tornado story as a whole to a close.

Fitted with a Vulture II rated at 1,760hp (1,312kW), the first prototype Tornado P5219 was built in the Kingston Experimental Shop. It was transported to Hawker's Langley aerodrome on 31 July 1939 and had its first engine run on 12 September. The aircraft began taxi trials at Langley on 1 October 1939 and Hawker test pilot Flt Lt Philip G Lucas performed the first flight on 6 October. Preliminary handling trials were made at an all-up weight of 9,127lb (4,140kg) and the aircraft was fitted with a 13.2ft-diameter (4.0m) Rotol airscrew.

The Tornado and Typhoon's wings were very thick (19.5% thickness-to-chord ratio at the root) and once either of these aircraft was put into a high-speed dive the effects of air compressibility would begin to appear. This resulted in a sudden sharp increase in drag in the region of 500mph (805kph) and the aircraft would become nose heavy (as a consequence the follow-on Tempest used a thinner wing). The early Tornado flight trials revealed evidence of the effects of compressibility on the airframe for the first time. The engine's radiator cowling had been placed under the fuselage near the wing/body junction, in a position similar to the Hurricane, but this proved unsatisfactory since vibration was experienced around the ventral radiator when the airspeed approached 400mph (644kph).

It was found that there were three separate systems of airflow in this region – one over the wings, one over the fuselage and one around the outside of the radiator cowling – with the result that they interfered with one another and produced very high local airflow velocities. This brought the onset

Considering that only four examples flew, there are a surprisingly large number of photographs available of the various Hawker Tornados. This view shows the first prototype P5219 in October 1939 at around the time of its maiden flight, with the original radiator position. (Crown Copyright)

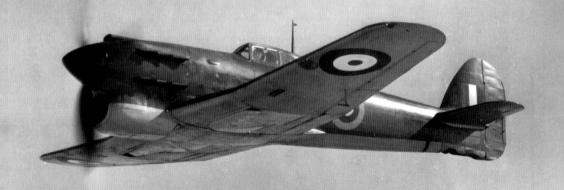

Above, below and opposite: This batch of recognition photos of the second Tornado prototype P5224 was taken on 3 October 1941 during its visit to A&AEE Boscombe Down. (Crown Copyright via Phil Butler)

of the effect of compressibility which resulted in a sudden sharp increase in drag coupled with a violent shuddering and vibration. Indeed photographs taken from a Hurricane flying underneath the Tornado showed that wool tufts attached to the rear half of the latter's radiator cowling were actually being moved forwards by the airflow. Moving the cowling to the position immediately under the engine cured the problem entirely although this required a considerable redesign. The first flight with P5219 incorporating the new arrangement took place on 6 December 1939 and tailwheel doors were subsequently added to improve the airflow even further.

The switch to a nose radiator also helped with engine cooling, but in addition the Tornado experienced unsatisfactory directional stability. Extra rudder area was provided to deal with this and Lucas took P5219 on its first flight with the larger fin and rudder on 16 May 1940 (the modified fin and rudder were also applied to the Typhoon prototype). In due course, P5219 spent some time based at Rolls-Royce's test airfield at Hucknall and eventually received a full armament of 12 machine guns. On 27 March 1941 the first Tornado began flying with a 1,980hp (1,476kW) Vulture V and it went on to enjoy a long career, being used entirely in trials and experimental work. On 23 June 1943 P5219 went de Havilland for more testing, before being Struck Off Charge and 'destroyed' at Hawkers in late August 1943.

The second prototype Tornado, P5224, flew from the start with a production Vulture II and the radiator in the forward position, and also had additional window panels to improve the rearwards view. The first flight was made on 5 December 1940 well over a year after P5219, which reflected the loss of priority that the Tornado had experienced since its flying programme had opened (in part due to the halt to the Typhoon and Tornado programmes ordered in May 1940).

In late August and through much of September 1941, P5224 was based at Hucknall, then on 1 October it went to the Aircraft & Armament Experimental Establishment (A&AEE) at Boscombe Down to undergo brief handling trials at a take-off weight of 10,690lb (4,849kg). A total of 30° of flap was used for take-off, with the tail trim set slightly forward of centre (ie, slightly nose heavy) and the rudder bias at half of the travel to the full-left position. There was a strong tendency for the aircraft to swing to the right even with half-left trim and this was most pronounced as full throttle was reached; the swing, however, could be held easily by applying rudder. Retracting the undercarriage produced a noticeable tail heaviness, which was easily held but did necessitate retrimming. Retraction of flap caused no noticeable change of trim, and there was sufficient rudder bias to trim the aircraft on the climb for 'feet-off' flight.

In general flight the Tornado prototype's controls were satisfactory and equal in all respects to those on the Typhoon, but the Tornado was considered more stable longitudinally than the Typhoon. All normal aerobatics were carried out without difficulty and dives were made up to 450mph (724kph) ASI (Airspeed Indicated). The aircraft proved to be very pleasant to fly in MS (Medium Supercharged) gear, but there was a very noticeable vibration in FS (Fully Supercharged) gear, which was at its worst with the engine at maximum power. By opening the throttle very slowly the engine could be made to run smoothly for about 30 secs before the vibration recommenced, the test pilot reporting that the vibration was very unpleasant and might in time have a serious effect on the Tornado's structure.

The Tornado's approximate stalling speeds were:

- Flaps and undercarriage up – 82mph (132kph) ASI.
- Flaps and undercarriage down – 61mph (98kph) ASI.

The stalling characteristics were similar to the Typhoon, but the actual speeds were lower by some margin. The best approach speed was 90mph (145kph) ASI and the landing itself was straightforward

The first production Tornado R7936 seen in its original form with a three-blade propeller. (Peter Green)

R7936 pictured again after the contra-rotating propeller (contraprop) had been fitted. The second view at least was taken at Staverton, Rotol's test airfield. (Rotol)

Left: Close-up of R7936's contraprop installation, a de Havilland photo that is dated 2 February 1943. Note again the twin rows of exhaust stubs. (Rotol)

Below and opposite: The only production Hawker Tornado to fly was indeed R7936. The head-on view of the aircraft in its original form was taken in October 1941. (Crown Copyright)

and easy, the characteristics being similar to the Typhoon. Overall, the report concluded that the Tornado's handling was 'indistinguishable from the Typhoon'.

During these trials P5224, now fitted with a 1,980hp (1,476kW) Vulture V, achieved a maximum rate of climb of 3,500ft/min up to 3,200ft and the aircraft took 7.2 mins to reach 20,000ft. Its service ceiling was 34,900ft. The maximum speed with 8lb/sq in (0.55 bar) boost (the maximum attainable during level-speed trials) was 398mph (641kph) at 23,300ft, but it was estimated that with the stipulated boost of 9lb/sq in (0.62 bar) the speed would be 400mph (644kph) at 22,500ft. Since it was a prototype P5224 did of course lack a lot of equipment, but ballast had been added to obtain the correct weight. Also, the wings had been adapted for 20mm cannon but these had not yet been fitted, so the leading-edge gun ports were covered over. Between 6 November 1941 and April 1943 P5224 was based at RAE Farnborough for diving trials and an assessment of 'rear-view mirror drag'. On 10 April it went into store, and was scrapped at No. 50 MU (Maintenance Unit) at Oxford after September 1944.

The first production Tornado, R7936, first became airborne from Avro's Woodford airfield on 29 August 1941. Similar to P5224 but without the rear window panels in a hood fairing, during autumn 1941 R7936 was flown by service pilots who were impressed with its performance and handling, but critical of the view to the rear. Used primarily for engine and propeller development, R7936 spent periods with Rolls-Royce, Rotol and then de Havilland Engines. On 8 March 1942 it joined Rolls-Royce to have a six-blade contra-rotating propeller (contraprop) fitted, the aircraft then joining Rotol at Staverton on 21 September for trials. On 21 December it went to de Havilland to begin trials with a DH six-blade contraprop. Reports indicate that the contraprop destabilised the aircraft markedly.

R7936 was delivered to No. 43 Group (Maintenance Command) for scrap in April 1944. After the cancellation of Tornado production, airframes R7937 and R7938 did not progress to full flying condition, although both were apparently near complete with the latter to be allocated to Rolls-Royce.

Bristol Centaurus Testbed

An additional Tornado prototype was built specifically to test the Bristol Centaurus 18-cylinder air-cooled radial engine. Fitting this engine had been considered in November 1939 when a mock-up installation was carried out on P5224 before its Vulture was installed, but this new project became part of the background work for the Centaurus-powered Tempest II fighter. The Bristol Aeroplane

Company's Engine Division specialised in air-cooled radial engines and its new Centaurus was a follow-on to the earlier Hercules. It was type-tested in 1938 but did not enter production until 1942.

The Centaurus installation was conventional and had a front exhaust-collector ring inside a lipped shroud, a single external exhaust pipe and a combined fairing for the carburettor intakes and the oil cooler. Bristol designed the new cowling ahead of the bulkhead while Hawker worked on the structural alterations required to enable a standard Tornado to receive a Centaurus. The engine mounting and the structure forward of the fireproof bulkhead had to be altered and the fuselage back to the cockpit needed re-skinning, but the remainder of the structure used existing parts. Hawker received the contract for this one-off aircraft on 22 February 1941 and the Ministry called the prototype the 'Centaurus-Typhoon'. However, Hawker rejected this name because, owing to its different forward fuselage structure, it would not have been possible to fit a Centaurus to a Typhoon body in the same way (see below).

Above, below and opposite: Walk-around views of the final Hawker Tornado to fly, the Bristol Centaurus engine testbed serial HG641. Here it has a three-blade propeller and a single exhaust pipe beneath the cowling, which passes under the wing leading edge. (Crown Copyright)

This final Tornado, serial HG641, had a newly built centre fuselage, a rear fuselage taken from the production line and an existing set of Tornado wings, and was fitted with a Centaurus IV CE.4.SM and three-blade Rotol constant-speed propeller. It was delivered to Langley almost complete on 22 September 1941 and from here Philip Lucas took it on its maiden flight on 23 October at an all-up weight of 10,320lb (4,681kg); there was no armament. Due to vibration HG641's early flight trials were unsatisfactory, the vibration apparently being due to disturbed airflow brought about by the close proximity of the exhaust pipe to the wing undersurface and the cooler fairing. A modification saw the single tail pipe set at 20° above the thrust line on the port side but the trouble persisted, and then a bearing failure on the supercharger brought flying in this configuration to a close.

In February 1942 it was decided to install a new fairing and twin exhaust pipe arrangement with the latter enclosed in a fairing on the cowling underside. The new form also saw the oil-cooler and

Above and left: HG641 later acquired a four-blade propeller and a much-modified lower cowling with a deeper lower section ahead of and blended into the wing. Images taken at Langley in November 1942. (Crown Copyright)

air intakes extended forward with the cowling redesigned completely. The aircraft also received an enlarged spinner, which fully enclosed the propeller hub. Finally, the Centaurus was fitted with a two-speed supercharger. This work was done at Kingston and in mid-November the modified aircraft went back to Langley to resume flying. In December HG641 began to make up for its bad start with a performance that showed some potential, a speed of 402mph (647kph) being recorded at 18,000ft.

On 3 February 1942 Rowe had told Hawker that the 'Centaurus-Typhoon' was to be developed as a matter of urgency, that six additional airframes were to be built (LA594, LA597, LA602, LA607, LA610 and LA614) and jigging and tooling was required for extensive production. The contract for these prototypes was received at Kingston on 23 March and it was agreed that they should have four-blade propellers.

However, on 12 May Camm explained to Rowe that it was impractical to install the Centaurus in the Typhoon itself, pointing out that the front wing spar was in the way of the engine, which was not the case on the Tornado or the Typhoon II (Typhoon II was the title first given to what would become the Tempest). So on 2 June the Centaurus-Typhoon programme was cancelled (some of the serials listed above were reused on Tempests). On 30 June the Typhoon II installation was given highest priority and from this point the Centaurus design effort moved on to what became the Tempest II.

Thus HG641 was the only Centaurus-powered Typhoon or Tornado to fly and it eventually went to Bristol Engines at Filton for further development work, Bristol test pilot Cyril Uwins making his firm's first flight in the aircraft on 8 March 1943. By 21 September HG641 had accumulated over 202 flying hours and this Tornado did much to help clear the Centaurus for service in the Tempest II. Finally, in August 1944 it was delivered to No. 43 Group (Maintenance Command) for scrapping. With the Centaurus in place HG641 was considered to be over-powered.

Vulture engine development brought problems with fatigue failures of some components, especially in the big-end bearings through fractures of the connecting-rod bolts. This affected the concurrent Avro Manchester bomber programme very badly since this aircraft used two Vultures and suffered repeated failures which resulted in the loss of numerous airframes. The Vulture was consequently abandoned, taking the Tornado and Manchester programmes with it. However, it should be stated that, although the Tornado progressed little further than prototype status, it is understood that the fighter experienced few problems with its own Vulture powerplant. A good deal of the aerodynamic trials flying conducted by those Tornados that were flown proved very beneficial to the Typhoon, and to the Centaurus powerplant for the Tempest.

Above left and above right: Three-quarter port angle views of HG641 in its two forms that show well the changes made to the engine installation after the first stage of flight testing. Note also the 12 gun ports in its later condition. (Hawker)

Chapter 3
Typhoon Flight Test

U nlike the Tornado, the two Typhoon prototypes, P5212 and P5216, featured a chin radiator from the start. Prototype P5212 was transported to Langley on 21 January 1940 and the first ground running of its Sabre engine took place on 1 February. The aircraft commenced its flight trials on 24 February with a de Havilland 14ft-diameter (4.3m) Hydromatic airscrew fitted and Philip Lucas in the cockpit. However, on 9 May when Lucas took P5212 on another test flight he experienced a failure in the rear-fuselage monocoque just behind the cockpit, where it was connected to the centre fuselage, which occurred while the aircraft was flying at 270mph (435kph) ASI and 10,500ft. Such was the danger of the situation that Lucas was fully entitled to bale out, but he stayed with the aircraft and landed safely, which ensured that Hawker's engineers could inspect the damaged airframe. For this heroism Lucas received the George Medal.

A&AEE Boscombe Down pilots carried out an interim review of P5212 at Langley between 26 September and 15 October 1940, most of the flying being done at a start weight of 10,620lb (4,817kg). By this time P5212 had the enlarged fin and rudder already flown on the Tornado. The aircraft had a 1,950hp (1,454kW) Sabre NS.1.SMb engine and gave a best rate of climb of 2,730ft/min at 15,500ft. The maximum level speed obtained with the supercharger in FS gear was 410mph (660kph) at nearly 20,000ft, while the provisional figure in MS gear was 396mph (637kph) at 8,000ft. The greatest height achieved was 29,500ft while the estimated service ceiling was about 32,000ft.

On take-off there was a marked tendency to swing to the right, especially when full throttle was reached, but this could be controlled by the rudder, which was moderately light and effective, and there was no difficulty in maintaining directional control once the aeroplane was airborne. When the undercarriage was raised with the flaps 30° down and radiator shutter open, a moderate tail heaviness was induced but no noticeable change of trim occurred when the flaps were raised. Closing the radiator

Typhoon EK497 was photographed on 18 September 1943 armed with rocket projectiles (RP) during A&AEE trials. (Crown Copyright)

Above and right:
R7579 was the fourth
production Typhoon
Mk IA built by Gloster
Aircraft and shows
the original canopy
fairing. The small
windows trialled on
the first prototype
had not been
adopted. (Phil Butler)

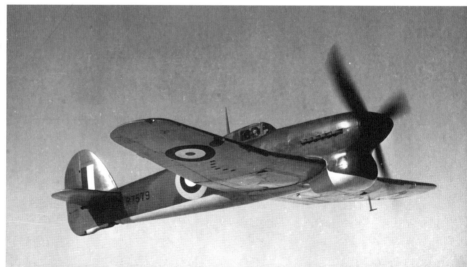

shutter made P5212 nose heavy. In level flight the aeroplane was sufficiently stable about all axes and the controls were light, effective and well harmonized throughout the very wide speed range. The aircraft banked more easily to the right than to the left, due, presumably, to the torque effect of the left-hand rotation of the airscrew, and there was no tendency for the aeroplane to tighten itself in a turn. The approximate stalling speeds were:

- Flaps and undercarriage up – 88mph (142kph) ASI.
- Flaps and undercarriage down – 70mph (113kph) ASI.

Several dives were made up to 475mph (764kph) ASI during which P5212 was steady with its behaviour described as 'very satisfactory'. The dives were made at 10,485lb (4,756kg) weight and the ailerons were found to be moderately light and sufficiently effective up to this speed, with no signs of overbalancing or snatching. The elevator and rudder controls were moderately light and well harmonised with the ailerons, there was no tendency for either wing to drop in the dive and the aeroplane could be held on a target. Lucas had made one dive at 505mph (813kph) ASI (at 10,621lb (4,818kg) weight) and found that the controls were still satisfactory at the higher speed. For landing the wheels were best lowered at a speed of about 160mph (257kph) ASI and this produced some fore-and-aft pitching which was, however, not serious. The flaps were fully lowered at about 140mph (225kph) ASI without any noticeable change of trim and the approach was best made at a speed of

approximately 100mph (161kph) ASI, with touch down at 72mph (116kph).

In conclusion P5212 was described as very pleasant to fly and, by then, no vices had been discovered. The report noted that the aircraft had well-harmonized controls and its high speed 'should make the aeroplane a very effective fighting machine'. The top speed represented 'an appreciable advance over current fighters' but there were some criticisms – the service ceiling was insufficient for the needs of the time, whilst the engine cooling was inadequate and needed to be increased. Again the rearward view also required improvement.

The second prototype P5216 first flew on 3 May 1941, but suffered a landing accident at Boscombe on 11 July when the port undercarriage collapsed inwards and the port wing hit the ground. On 7 November P5216 was cleared for flight with extended wing tips in an effort to increase the type's ceiling. The first production Typhoon R7576 was flown on 26 May 1941 at Gloster complete with machine-gun armament. Hawker Langley's first production Typhoon, R8199, first flew on 26 November 1941 and soon the 'screaming' noise associated with the Sabre power unit was becoming very familiar to those living in the areas surrounding Duxford and Brockworth.

One attempt at increasing the Typhoon's rudder area is shown here with extensions to the trailing edge.

Such was the poor visibility from certain parts of the canopy that a campaign was launched to develop something better, a point pushed particularly strongly by Sqn Ldr R P Beamont who in 1942 carried out a lot of production test flying for Hawker. Although the 'solid' rear portion of the canopy was now transparent, the heavy framing still restricted vision. The resulting introduction of a one-piece blown 'tear-drop' Perspex hood proved to be a vast improvement over the original canopy and gave the pilot a remarkably unrestricted view. This was test-flown on R8809 with the prototype conversion being completed in January 1943, but the new form did not arrive on the production line until late that year. The last 'car-door' Typhoons left the front line soon after D-Day but a few examples were still flying in the hands of training units at the close of the war. An early attempt to improve the rearwards vision had been a rear-view mirror fitted in a small Perspex blister on the roof of the canopy.

Between 10 and 20 January 1944 JR333 was at Boscombe for handling trials. This aircraft was representative of the latest production version including the new sliding hood, but it still sported a three-blade propeller. When diving the aircraft to 480mph (772kph) ASI, and with it trimmed for all-out level flight, the pilot found the characteristics to be normal, and he concluded that the sliding hood had made no appreciable change to the Typhoon's handling characteristics.

In 1943 three Typhoons were sent to North Africa for tropical trials. Serials R8891, DN323 and EJ906 were taken from the Gloster line and then modified by Hawker for use in the Middle East. The main alteration was the introduction of a filter for air cleaning mounted inside a fairing behind the radiator under the fuselage. This was to be operated during ground running, taxiing, take-off and landing, the pilot switching back to the normal inlet during the flight itself.

The three aircraft arrived by ship at Casablanca on 25 April 1943 and after assembly were flown to No. 451 Fighter-Bomber Squadron at Idku in Egypt to begin a long series of intensive trials. Most of the flying was made from El Daba and the experiment lasted until October, proving the concept of using the Typhoon in tropical conditions. In the event, however, such was the need for the type in the European theatre that no examples could ever be spared for desert service and so the type would never operate there.

One of the three Typhoons to visit the Middle East for a series of intensive tropical trials. The aircraft is pictured in Egypt during its test flying programme. (Newark Air Museum)

Unusual photo of a Typhoon with its forward fuselage sealed off, presumably for carbon monoxide contamination tests. The aircraft was at the time apparently in the hands of Napier. (Phil Butler)

Below, opposite and page 36: One of the first production Typhoons to be tested at Boscombe Down was R7700 seen here in a series of recognition views made by A&AEE. Compared to R7579 this aircraft now has clear panelling in the rear canopy. (Crown Copyright via Phil Butler)

Returning to the early clearance flying, production Typhoon R7700, fitted with four 20mm cannon and a 14ft-diameter (4.3m) three-blade de Havilland Hydromatic propeller, was used by A&AEE in the summer of 1942 for climb- and level-speed-performance measurements. At a weight of 11,070lb (5,021kg) it showed a maximum rate of climb in MS gear of 2,790ft/min at 6,300ft and in FS gear 2,000ft/min at 17,800ft. The time taken to reach 25,000ft was 12.4 mins, the estimated service ceiling was 32,300ft and estimated absolute ceiling 33,000ft. The maximum true level speed in MS gear was 376mph (605kph) at 8,500ft and in FS gear 394mph (634kph) at 20,200ft.

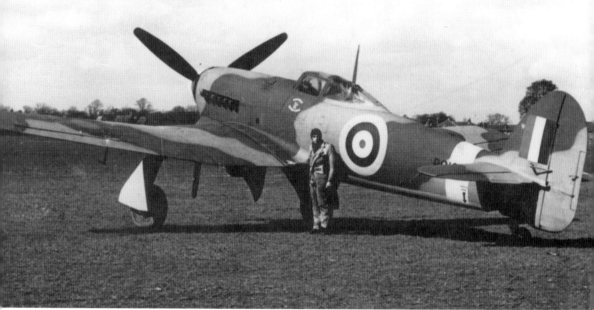

Above: R8198 was the first of the 15 Typhoons to be built by Hawker at Langley. Note the heavily framed 'car-door' canopy. (Peter Green)

Below: This Gloster-built Typhoon shows the early production form with three-blade propeller, 'car-door' canopy and the underwing identity stripes introduced at the end of 1942 to help Allied pilots and anti-aircraft gunners distinguish the Typhoon from the German Fw 190. (Jet Age Museum)

Another early series Mk IB Typhoon pictured in January 1943, here carrying 44 gal drop tanks and also with unfaired cannon. (Crown Copyright)

Lovely image of two Typhoons taken apparently prior to delivery. EK288 was a presentation aircraft and has 'Fiji VI' written just beneath the forward canopy. (Jet Age Museum)

After Camm had requested four-blade propellers for the Typhoon in July 1941, one de Havilland and one Rotol propeller were allocated for trials. The de Havilland propeller was received at Langley for test on 29 September and in due course the four-blader would become standard for the Typhoon. It was introduced to overcome vibration, which was experienced in conjunction with the Sabre's flexible engine mounting, and also to improve the take-off after the aircraft had been adapted to carry two 1,000lb (454kg) bombs. Early on there were troubles with vibration from the four-blade arrangement.

Another early problem to be solved was the flame-damping qualities of the Typhoon's exhaust system. The original arrangement consisted of six backward-facing stub pipes positioned close to the engine-cowling panel. It was found that this type of manifold produced a dangerous concentration of carbon monoxide in the aircraft, so a 4in (10cm) extension piece was inserted in each stub pipe taking the actual orifice 6in (15cm) away from the engine cowling panel. Flame-damping trials were conducted on both types of manifold using R7579 for the short stubs (in December 1941) and R7617

Right and overleaf:
In the spring of 1943 the aviation press visited Gloster's Hucclecote/ Brockworth facility to view the Typhoon. The images produced from this event show EK286 piloted by test pilot John Crosby Warren, who at the time was in charge of Typhoon production testing.

This Central Press photo was the one of the first pictures of 'the RAF's newest fighter, the Typhoon' to be released. A note on the back added that 'it was not to be published before 29 April 1943'. In fact this is almost certainly a 56 Squadron aircraft pictured on 21 April (note the black rear of the spinner). And the identity markings have been applied incorrectly, with one black and one white stripe short on each wing. (Peter Green)

for the longer variety (July 1942). The short stubs satisfied the required conditions except when viewed from three-quarter front, but the long-stub ejector pipes satisfied the required conditions completely, namely that neither exhaust flame nor glow should be visible from any direction under all engine conditions from a distance greater than 100 yards (91m).

Fuselage Failures

The most serious problem to afflict the Typhoon, and never truly solved, was the failure and detachment of the tailplane and end fuselage on a number of airframes, and in the majority of cases with the tragic loss of the pilot. The first three accidents brought about by structural failure occurred in quick succession, to R8633 at High Ercall on 29 July 1942, R7692 at Langley on 11 August and R7644 at Holbeach on 18 August. Between 24 October 1942 and 5 May 1943 there were eight further structural failures of Typhoons in the air, all of which were found to be broadly analogous to the previous cases. Of the eight aircraft concerned, four had received full modifications (described later) to the rear end.

On 12 August 1942 Hawker and Air Ministry representatives discussed the first two failures with scientists at RAE Farnborough. The two accidents exhibited similar features in that both had suffered an upward failure of one side of the fuselage, port in one aircraft and starboard in the other, with the failure at the joint between the replaceable tail-portion end and the monocoque rear half of the fuselage. A few days later came the third accident to R7644 and in all three cases the tail unit had parted from the rear fuselage at the aft transport joint, the elevator mass-balance weight within the fuselage had broken away, and the tailplane on one side had broken off in upload.

As a result RAE began a major programme of strength testing on the Typhoon airframe. In addition, strain gauges were to be fitted to the tailplane spars and the fin post to measure the stresses at the roots, so that it would be possible to deduce the bending moments and, hence, to establish the torsion on the fuselage and the fin and tailplane loads. Flutter was another possibility and extensive tests were also

JP853 pictured after having joined an RAF unit, as 'SA-K' of 486 Squadron. (Peter Green)

made in this area (flutter is the potentially dangerous oscillation of an aircraft or part of an aircraft brought about by the interaction of aerodynamic forces, structural elastic reactions and inertia – the the same set of conditions that make a flag flutter in a stiff breeze). In the meantime, Hawker had designed a modified rear transport joint, with the surrounding fuselage being strengthened, and had also modified the elevator mass-balance-weight assembly. In the very short term, a steel strap was inserted around the rear fuselage, and then in November 1942 tail-strengthening modifications were introduced, which required each individual Typhoon to return to the works for about a week.

Between 8 and 15 October 1942 R7577 was used for handling tests to assess modifications carried out on the combined rudder trimmer and balance tab, its chord having been increased from 4.625in/11.748cm to 5.875in/14.923cm (the length of the tab was unchanged). Normally full left rudder trim had to be used for take-off, but using this new setting it was found that there was no appreciable tendency for the Typhoon to swing during the take-off run, and any deviation from the chosen direction was easily checked. In general, on examples fitted with the standard type of rudder and rudder tab there was a considerable change in directional trim with changes in speed and power. That normally necessitated constant retrimming to relieve the pilot's foot loads, but on R7577 with the modified tab, the rudder had been lightened to such an extent that retrimming was not necessary. Overall, the modification to the rudder tab had improved the aircraft's directional control considerably and its adoption was recommended.

At one point it looked as if the fuselage problem had been solved, but an accident to R7695 in October 1942 proved otherwise. This failure, however, just forward of the tail unit and showing characteristics of the earlier accidents, had not involved a failure of the elevator mass-balance assembly in its modified form. As a result the previous explanation for the problem was no longer valid. In addition, the measurements of tail load in aerobatics, instituted at RAE as a necessary part of the investigation, had now provided evidence of tailplane loadings more severe than had been expected, chiefly in the recovery from a dive with high acceleration. Large differences in load on the port and starboard sides were noted and, since the loads

Below and overleaf: This Typhoon Mk IB JP682 was photographed on 24 August 1943. Note how the censor has blanked out the serial number on the side of the fuselage. (Peter Green)

R7695 was one of the Typhoons to experience fuselage failure.

were higher than expected, so the safety factor was below that previously thought to be present. A general strengthening of the rear fuselage was therefore required to counter these higher loads.

There was also a very marked vibration at the rear end of the aeroplane and on 27 October 1942 N E Rowe recommended a temporary restriction to 400mph (644kph) ASI (RAE was researching the vibration problem with the highest urgency). However, the restriction was rejected by Air Marshall F J Linnell, the Controller of Research and Development (CRD) at MAP, who wrote: 'The Typhoon is performing a most valuable role in Fighter Command operations and the imposition of a restriction such as that recommended would either be disregarded, or would detract seriously from the value of the Typhoon in its present special role'. The risk was accepted and no restrictions were therefore implemented.

Three more crashes occurred in January 1943 and all had the same problem of failure of the rear fuselage near the rear transport joint. By now the investigation had discovered that:

1. Estimates for flutter speed for the fuselage and tail unit had given a critical speed far outside the flying range, so flutter could not now be regarded as a possible cause.
2. The load measured on the tailplane in wind-tunnel tests and in flight, though more severe than expected both in amount and in asymmetry, was not alone sufficient to cause failure of the fuselage.

Modification-strengthening of the fuselage was now being applied as soon as possible to aircraft in service and in production, which in tests gave an increase in overall fuselage strength of 20% under loads on fin and rudder. By 30 January 1943 the number of Typhoons delivered was about 700, and the number in actual service was thought to be about 400, so the upgrading was a considerable task. Despite the long and very broad series of investigations, with all Typhoons receiving the strengthened rear airframe, in the end the fuselage failure problem was never fully cured. Aircraft were still lost from this weakness during 1944, and indeed Fg Off Eagles, a veteran of 198 Squadron, died just a few days after VE-Day in May 1945 when his Typhoon broke up near Brockenhurst during propeller trials for de Havilland. This tragedy was the last such occurrence.

During the test flying to try to establish the cause of the fuselage failures, pilots in the Typhoon began to encounter compressibility, a phenomenon already seen (and referred to) on the Tornado. Here the airflow accelerated locally in the regions of the wings and other fairings was being compressed as it approached the speed of sound, which created turbulence around the airframe, either as vibration or in the more severe cases buffeting. There would also be changes of trim with violent nose-up or nose-down pitching and, thus, some loss of control, the controls themselves becoming much heavier. This of course was happening when the Typhoon was in a dive, at heights roughly between 10,000ft and 25,000ft. As noted, it was the fighter's very thick wing that was the real problem.

In February 1943 a Typhoon was flown with a 13% increase in tailplane area, then on 25 October 1943 a Ministry memorandum referred to troubles with the Typhoon's longitudinal stability. The results of tests performed by Hawker with different balance weights on Typhoon and Tempest tailplanes, and with three- and four-blade propellers, brought the following suggestions:

1. For a Typhoon with the present standard tailplane and three-blade propeller – provide an 8lb (3.6kg) balance weight and 16lb (7.3kg) inertia weight on all aircraft in service and in production.
2. With the introduction of the four-blade propeller, the tailplane should be changed to the Tempest format and the mass-balance weight changed to 7lb (3.2kg) with an inertia weight of 16lb (7.3kg).

On 26 September 1943 Philip Lucas reported on some flights in EK229 then newly fitted with a standard set of Tempest-type tailplane and elevators. This modification was intended to counter the unsatisfactory characteristics of a standard Typhoon when fitted with increased mass-balanced elevators. Tests were performed at both 10,000ft and 20,000ft and the standard Tempest tailplane and elevators, with a standard 4.5lb (2kg) elevator mass balance, were found to have a slightly higher margin of both static and dynamic stability over that of a standard Typhoon, particularly at high altitudes. At 10,000ft the aircraft was stable in turns and did not tighten up. After further flight testing it was decided that the Tempest-type tailplane and elevators should be fitted to all Typhoon aircraft in production and retrospectively, which again proved to be a substantial task.

Engine Problems

Early in the Typhoon's career it became clear that the Napier Sabre did not supply sufficient power at high altitudes. Consequently, to try to improve the fighter's high-altitude performance, test flights were made during 1941 using Typhoons with both extended and clipped wings, but to no avail (these changes also brought a loss of performance in other areas).

In addition, the early Typhoons experienced many engine problems, a situation highlighted by airframe production getting ahead of engine production, to the point where Gloster Aircraft had to ferry new examples to Maintenance Units using 'slave' engines, which were then taken out of these Typhoons, returned to Gloster and installed in the next batch of completed airframes while the earlier machines went into store. The engine shortage was exacerbated by frequent failures in service, especially through seizures of the sleeve valves. At the start the prototype engines had been hand-assembled by Napier's craftsmen, but the Sabre did not adapt well to the techniques of assembly-line production. In particular the sleeves often failed, leading to seized cylinders, which resulted in very short time periods between inspections (just 25 hours at the end of 1942). As a result, operational

Typhoon squadrons had to have their monthly flying limited to 300 hours for fighter units and 200 hours for fighter-bombers.

Eventually, after consultations with the Bristol Engine Company, and the testing of a large number of different materials and manufacturing techniques, Napier was able to introduce a process of nitriding and 'lapping' for the Sabre sleeves, which solved most of the problems. As a result engine serviceability quickly rose to an acceptable level (at the same time the manufacturer's standards of quality control were improved).

These problems almost brought the withdrawal of the Typhoon from Fighter Command, but the arrival of German 'hit-and-run' raiders provided a lifeline because the Typhoon was fast enough to deal with these. With the improvements outlined above the fighter began to record some success which ensured that it would stay in the inventory. With refinements to the design, increased power and the adoption of the engine in the Tempest as well, the reputation of the Sabre would eventually rise to a high level, which at war's end was thoroughly deserved.

Trials for Operational Service

Experiments to prepare the Typhoon for use as a fighter-bomber began in August 1942 when R7646 had bomb racks fitted under each wing. During the subsequent trials it was found that putting 500lb (227kg) bombs on underwing racks did not lower the Typhoon's top speed by very much, but the extra weight did reduce the rate of climb somewhat since the wing loading had been increased. Handling tests with a 500-pounder under each wing were undertaken at A&AEE using R7646, now with fairings fitted around the bomb racks. Except in the dive, the bombs had little effect on the aircraft's handling, but there was buffet at speeds above 350mph (563kph), although the aircraft remained steady up to the limiting speed of 400mph (644mph). Without the bomb rack fairings the aircraft pitched in a dive although this could be controlled.

Rocket-projectile (RP) installation trials were first performed using Mk IB EK497 between 23 July and 24 September 1943. A speed of 285mph (459kph) ASI was found to be the most suitable for level attack and, although at this stage the installation was non-standard, the aircraft used in the A&AEE trials attained a high degree of accuracy for rocket firing and was found to be an excellent 'platform' for this type of work. Introducing the rocket to the front line, however, required a lot of airframe modifications plus a new training programme in the techniques for using the weapon. In service the normal load was eight RPs, but on some occasions a 12-rocket configuration was employed on operations with double rockets on the inner pairs of rails. In August 1944 MN861 was flown by A&AEE with a 16-rocket load (double rockets on all rails) and the Establishment's pilots reported satisfactory handling including during dives at 450mph (724kph) ASI. However, when the Air Fighting Development Unit (AFDU), based at the time at Wittering, assessed the 16-rocket load on EK290 they found that the Typhoon now had a very long take-off run, its climb was poor and the top speed attained was just 310mph (499kph) at 3,000ft. Consequently, this configuration was never used on operations.

In December 1942 and January 1943, Mk IB R8762 was fitted with two 44 gal (200l) drop tanks under the wings outboard of the undercarriage and was tested by A&AEE to determine their effect on the aircraft's performance. The 20mm cannon had their muzzles sealed and the take-off weight was 11,855lb (5,377kg) (the weight with full service equipment and full fuel). The performance was measured in a climb up to 30,000ft with the radiator flaps open, the climb being made at 185mph (298kph) ASI up to 16,000ft and decreasing by 3mph (4.8kph) per 1,000ft above that height.

The maximum rate of climb in MS gear was 2,630ft/min at 5,300ft and in FS gear 1,790ft/min at 16,000ft. The time taken to reach 10,000ft was 4.1 mins and 20,000ft 10.1 mins, the estimated service

Gloster's factory in summer 1943 showing a Typhoon with a newly completed bubble canopy conversion (protected by a cover), and with 'car-door' versions undergoing the same process in the background. The lack of forward fuselage panelling has revealed the complexity of the airframe and the equipment fitted within. (Jet Age Museum)

Below and opposite top: Photos showing MN235 (now in the RAF Museum) at Wright Field in the USA for trials. It has the new canopy and a three-blade propeller. (Peter Green)

Opposite bottom: RB363 testing the carriage of supply containers at the Airborne Forces Experimental Establishment (AFEE) at Beaulieu early in 1945. These were used to drop supplies to the SAS behind German lines shortly before the end of the war. (Chris Thomas)

Above: MN186 pictured during pre-delivery flight testing at Brockworth.

Left and below: R7646 was one of the first Typhoons with the clear canopy fairing, and was retained by Hawker for development work. It later undertook bomb carrying trials for A&AEE Boscombe Down. (Crown Copyright)

ceiling was 29,600ft and the estimated absolute ceiling 30,400ft. In level flight, the maximum level true airspeed was measured at 343.5mph (553kph) at 7,200ft in MS gear and 359.5mph (579kph) at 18,800ft in FS gear. The extra fuel in the 44 gal (200l) tanks extended the range by over 50% and 90 gal (409l) tanks would in due course become available.

In April 1943 A&AEE tested DN340 with a 1,000lb (454kg) bomb under each wing. R7646 with two 500lb (227kg) bombs (above) had been limited to 400mph (644kph) ASI in a dive, so the limiting speed on DN340 with its two 1,000-pounders was taken as the same (trials completed in March 1944 allowed the limit with two 500lb bombs to be raised to 450mph/724kph ASI). Some vibration was experienced at speeds above 290mph (467kph) ASI, which increased slightly with speed, but this was not in any way dangerous. Behaviour in the dive was satisfactory and the control characteristics at all speeds were good. Brief handling tests carrying just one 1,000-pounder showed that at moderate and fast speeds the aircraft was laterally out of trim but the aileron forces required to keep the aircraft level were not large. The force required did increase with a decrease in speed, and at speeds below 150mph (241kph) ASI a strong force on the control column was needed. At 140mph (225kph) ASI a large aileron movement and a heavy force on the control column were necessary, so the speed was not reduced further when carrying a single bomb. In all cases the bombs were dropped prior to landing, and overall the aircraft's handling characteristics with two 1,000lb (454kg) bombs were considered satisfactory.

The climb rating for the Sabre II was increased during the first months of 1943 and in May R8762 was used to measure the new rates of climb. A&AEE found that the extra power gave a maximum rate of climb of 3,380ft/min at 4,100ft in MS gear and 2,310ft/min at 16,800ft in FS gear; the estimated service ceiling was now 33,300ft. Late in the war, AFDU undertook trials with napalm tanks under the wings up to 1,000lb (454kg) in weight. These were not a total success and it was found that their release had to be made at low altitude, but on 12 April 1945 eight aircraft of 193 Squadron successfully used napalm in an attack on a German strongpoint near Arnhem. In early 1944 JR307 was used by A&AEE to test the use of M10 smoke tanks for laying a smoke-screen, a role in which the aircraft proved successful. This was part of the preparations for D-Day, but on the day itself the Typhoon squadrons had so many offensive operations to perform that any smoke-laying had to be carried out by Douglas Bostons.

AFDU Evaluation

The Air Fighting Development Unit (AFDU) based at Duxford conducted 'tactical trials' with a Typhoon. The resulting report was dated 30 October 1941 and included the following notes.

In terms of its flying characteristics the aircraft was pleasant to fly and easy to land. The take-off was reasonably short but the aircraft tended to swing to starboard, and when throttling back prior to making the approach to landing it was found that the engine had an unpleasant flat spot which caused 'cutting'. This had occurred at comparatively high revs and low boost, but the engine fired again as soon as the throttle was opened. This was considered to be most unsatisfactory, but it was understood that Napier had been instructed to rectify the fault as soon as possible since it was prevalent in all of the Sabre II engines.

In the air the controls were well-balanced and comparatively light, and at speeds above 400mph (644kph) ASI there was little tendency to 'heavy-up', the elevators still being pleasantly light. The Typhoon had been dived up to 480mph (772kph) ASI and, although the aircraft tended to turn to the left at this speed, it could easily be kept straight by use of rudder bias. In an operational climb with full throttle and maximum revs (3,700rpm), the rate of climb fell away to 500ft/min at 31,500ft. It was considered that the operational ceiling for a squadron of these aircraft would be about 26,000ft, at which height the controls were still good and the maximum speed high. The aircraft behaved normally in aerobatics, but the pilot was conscious of flying a fighter that was heavier than contemporary types. Again, the all-round view from the cockpit was not good, especially to the rear, and in formation the aircraft was simple to handle, although its deceleration was poor owing to its clean lines.

The aircraft's manoeuvrability in dogfighting was compared with a Supermarine Spitfire Mk VB at heights between 15,000ft and 26,000ft, with both aircraft carrying a full war load. The Typhoon, although not quite as manoeuvrable as the Spitfire, could get in a good burst during the initial stages of a turn. However, during turns it was found that the Spitfire could always turn more tightly than the Typhoon and that, if the Typhoon was behind, the Spitfire could get on to the Typhoon's tail after about two complete turns. Use was made of the Typhoon's superior speed and consequent high initial rate of climb to get away from the Spitfire and obtain a height advantage. The Typhoon could then carry out continued diving attacks, similar to those adopted by the German Messerschmitt Bf 109F, and use the speed obtained in the dive to break away to regain an advantage in height.

The AFDU pilots stressed that it must be remembered that indicated air speeds of over 400mph (644kph) could be obtained quickly when diving the Typhoon, and that the closing speed was greater than in contemporary types. The aircraft must, therefore, be ready to take evasive action as it might easily overshoot its target. Similarly, if fighting near the ground, the pilot had to be careful when diving steeply as the height required to pull out was considerable.

At 26,000ft altitude it was found that steep turns to the right were more satisfactory than to the left, probably due to torque. To the right a sustained turn of 4G or more was comfortable, whereas when turning steeply to the left with much less 'G' the turn tightened itself and the aircraft eventually flicked over to the right, losing about 2,000ft. Below 20,000ft the Typhoon was good in all turns and combat manoeuvres, but severe vibration of the airframe was apparent in steep turns of over 4G.

When being attacked from above, it was found that the best evasive manoeuvre was a steep climbing turn towards the Spitfire as it came into range, providing that the Typhoon was utilising its high cruising speed. If the Typhoon was cruising at a low speed, the best evasive manoeuvre was a steep diving turn towards the opposing fighter as it came into range, at the same time opening the throttle fully to obtain maximum speed quickly. It was found that the Typhoon could out-dive the Spitfire with ease and could break off the combat as desired in order to regain a tactical advantage of height. However, the poor view to the rear was a great disadvantage during dogfights and it was essential to use the utmost vigilance to avoid being 'jumped'. Against a bomber target, the Typhoon was able to deliver good quarter and astern attacks provided the target's speed was in excess of 160mph (257kph); at lesser speeds the Typhoon was in difficulty because of the fast closing speed.

The Spitfire engaged in dog-fighting the Typhoon found that, at 200 yards (183m) slightly below the Typhoon, the slipstream was so strong that it made accurate sighting extremely difficult. Although the Typhoon pilot's view was poor, low flying in good visibility presented no difficulty; however, in bad visibility, due to the high speed of the aircraft and restricted forward view, this became unpleasant.

In conclusion, the report stated that the Typhoon I was about 40mph (64kph) faster than the Spitfire VB at all heights above 14,000ft, and below this height it was even faster. The true top speed of the Typhoon Mk I was around 412mph (663kph) at 20,500ft, and the operational ceiling was 26,000ft. The aircraft behaved normally in aerobatics, but its all-round view from the cockpit was poor and this disadvantage was keenly felt when searching and dogfighting. The Typhoon was not quite as manoeuvrable as the Spitfire VB, but the method used to attack an aircraft was similar to the Spitfire – ie, carry out short diving attacks and then use the Typhoon's superior speed to regain height for further attacks.

An example of a Spitfire Mk VB that was used by the Air Fighting Development Unit to perform mock combats against a Typhoon. In this way some of the new aircraft's strengths and weaknesses could be determined. (Crown Copyright)

Above and overleaf: After a modification programme at Hawker Aircraft in May 1944, Typhoon Mk IB JR128, with bubble canopy, was used to produce a series of publicity pictures. It retains code letters HF-L, the markings of previous owner 183 Squadron. (Hawker Aircraft)

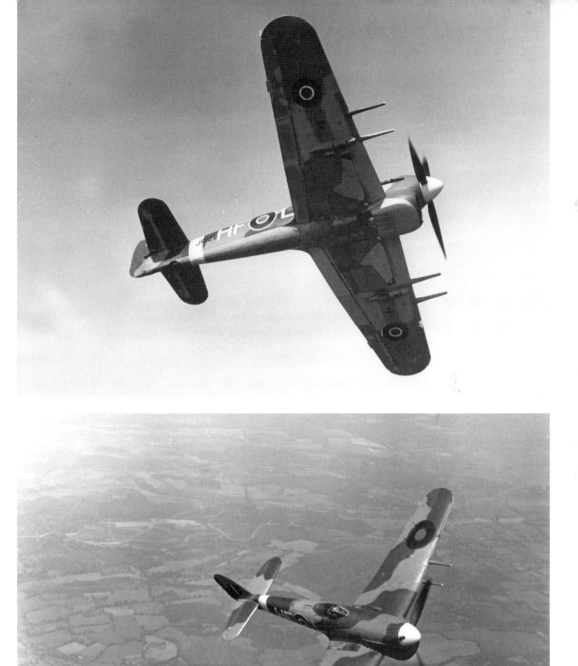

Photos of production Typhoons taken at Gloster's Brockworth factory. The lower view shows JR492 in the production standard of December 1943, and it has the identity stripes that were carried until 7 February 1944. The upper aircraft is very similar, but has no stripes, so dating it after 7 February 1944. It is probably an early MN-series aircraft. (Jet Age Museum)

'Spotters Day'! A Gloster-built Typhoon passes over the *Aeroplane* magazine's photographer on 23 August 1945. (Jet Age Museum)

The procession to mark the last Typhoon to be manufactured at the Hucclecote factory, which is believed to have taken place on 11 September 1945. (Jet Age Museum)

Gloster photo showing many of the people responsible for producing the Typhoon at its factories. Gloster general manager Frank McKenna is in the centre wearing the overcoat, chief test pilot Eric Greenwood stands second from McKenna to his right, test pilot Llewellyn Moss is second from McKenna on his left, and production test pilot Sqn Ldr Philip J Stanbury DFC is immediately to Moss's left in the RAF uniform. (Jet Age Museum)

Another photo of the last Typhoon to be produced by Gloster, SW772, in November 1945. Standing in front (left to right) are Eric Greenwood, Frank McKenna and Llewellyn Moss, the last a production test pilot on Typhoons and Gloster Meteor jet fighters. Moss subsequently lost his life in a Meteor. (Jet Age Museum)

Chapter 4

Typhoon Operations: UK

This narrative has been written using several sources but specific credit must go to the most important published account, the volume written by Chris Thomas and Christopher Shores called *The Typhoon and Tempest Story*. This splendid work provides a vast amount of factual information taken from squadron diaries and many other official and original sources.

Defensive Roles

The first squadron to convert to the Hawker Typhoon was 56 in September 1941, the first example being delivered to that unit at Duxford on 11 September. The first job was to get the type fully operational, but at this early stage that proved impossible because of the teething troubles outlined in previous chapters, which meant that 56 Squadron remained non-operational until 30 May 1942. Plans to use the new fighter in cross-Channel 'Circus' and 'Ramrod' types of operation had to go on hold. 'Circus' referred to daylight missions where a light bomber squadron with strong fighter escort would make short forays against coastal targets in occupied Europe. 'Ramrod' had single or paired fighters using low cloud cover to attack enemy targets with machine-gun and cannon fire.

The Typhoon, and particularly its Sabre engine, had been rushed into service and was just not ready, with the technical and development problems continuing into and through 1943. In addition, it was pretty clear that the aircraft exhibited a relatively poor performance at altitude, and it lacked some manoeuvrability for air-to-air fighting (although events would later prove that the Typhoon was quite happy dogfighting enemy aircraft).

British official photograph of R8884/'HF-L' of 183 Squadron taken in 1943. (Crown Copyright)

Code 'Z-Z' was given to R7698, the mount of Wg Cdr Denys Gillam who was the Duxford Wing Leader in 1942. (Peter Green)

Typhoon IA of 197 Squadron, R7681/'OV-Z', fitted with 12 0.303in machine guns. It is seen flying in early 1943, not long after its white nose had been painted over, and was used for conversion training only.

This aircraft belongs to 182 Squadron but still has 56 Squadron markings. It is pictured at Martlesham Heath in September 1942. (Peter Green)

The Squadron's conversion was hit by the loss of an aircraft and its pilot on 1 November 1941 when the Typhoon dived into the ground. The cause proved to be carbon monoxide exhaust gases reaching the cockpit and, although modifications were made to the sealing, in future Typhoon pilots would always use their oxygen masks in flight (the port-side cockpit doors were also now permanently sealed). Typhoons were also lost due to engine failure and other problems.

266 (Rhodesian) Squadron began to convert in January 1942, the unit's move to Duxford permitting the formation of the Duxford Wing along with 56 Squadron. In April 609 Squadron began to convert at Duxford when 266 Squadron moved to Snailwell. The first operational sortie was made on 30 May when eight 56 Squadron machines were despatched to intercept incoming 'Jagdbomber' (fighter-bomber) Focke-Wulf Fw 190s and Messerschmitt Bf 109s. Sadly, three days later two 56 Squadron Typhoons were shot down in error by Spitfires, their pilots mistaking the Typhoons for Fw 190s, while losses due to mechanical problems began to mount. In the meantime 257 and 486 Squadrons converted to the Typhoon as the pace of re-equipping accelerated. On 9 August 1942 two 266 Squadron aircraft downed a Junkers Ju 88 over the North Sea off Norfolk; the Typhoon's first air-to-air kill.

It is understood that the existence of the Typhoon was first revealed to the public after it flew in support of the raid on Dieppe on 19 August 1942, Operation *Jubilee*, the entire Duxford Wing of three squadrons taking part. In providing a fighter 'umbrella' for the landings, this proved to be Fighter Command's biggest single day of operations of the entire war as the Luftwaffe also became involved in strength. One Dornier Do 217 bomber was shot down by Typhoons along with a probable Fw 190, but the Wing took some losses during the three sorties it completed over the battle area. The introduction of yellow bands on the wings was the first attempt to help friendly fighters identify the newcomer. These were extended to multiple bands and then to an all-white nose, the latter most unpopular with the Typhoon pilots when it was introduced on 19 November 1942 (the white nose was abandoned on 5 December).

Above left and above right: R8220 was one of the few Typhoons built by Hawker's Langley factory and is pictured undergoing engine maintenance while serving with 56 Squadron as 'US-D'. Although listed as a Mk IA with machine guns, cannon had been fitted by the time these photographs were taken. The engine covers rest against the wing. The maintenance crew has stopped to watch an approaching aircraft, probably a Lockheed Hudson, flying at extremely low level! Hope the CO was not watching as well!

Below: Groundcrew manoeuvre a 56 Squadron Typhoon at Matlask, one of Fighter Command's grass airfields, on 21 April 1943.

Two views of R8224 taken in November 1942 when the aircraft had just had its nose painted white. (Peter Green)

The white-nose identity scheme and car-door cockpit are displayed by R8895, which joined 182 Squadron at Martlesham in December 1942. (Peter Green)

Previously, on 20 June, 56 and 266 Squadrons working together had made their first sweep over enemy territory as the Typhoon began to be used for ground-attack and anti-shipping missions. To prevent an example falling into enemy hands, however, pilots flying over enemy-held territory were advised to bale out rather than attempt a forced landing. From November 56 Squadron's aircraft carried bombs, and from February 1944 rockets, to enable them to attack airfields in France then in March 1944 56 Squadron began to re-equip with Spitfires.

After Dieppe the Duxford Wing was broken up as the Typhoon squadrons, now including 181 and 182, were spread around the southern counties to provide air defence. These new units, however, were to operate as fighter-bomber squadrons (see later), though the Typhoon was to enjoy nearly a year of success as a pure fighter. On 6 September 1944, two Messerschmitt Me 210s were shot down, and on 14 September, 56 Squadron made its first kill with a Ju 88. On 17 October a 'hit-and-run' Fw 190 was destroyed by aircraft from 486 Squadron, the first such success for the Typhoon, and 257 Squadron got two more on 3 November with 609 Squadron shooting down or damaging several more during the month.

Next, on 17 November 1944, 609 Squadron made its first night 'Rhubarb' sortie over France, and that same day 56 Squadron made a daylight 'Rhubarb' using gunfire to attack Bf 109s based near Vlissingen. 'Rhubarb' was an operation in which sections of fighters or fighter-bombers used poor visibility and low cloud to cross the Channel unseen and then searched for targets of opportunity, and they became more frequent during the winter. During December 1942 at least 11 enemy aircraft were shot down by Typhoons over or near southern England.

The Typhoon's UK air-defence role continued in 1943 and now included standing patrols specifically to deal with incoming raiders, a task known as 'anti-Rhubarbs'. The fuselage failures and Sabre problems continued but were kept under control, the engines having to be fully overhauled after just 25 hours; to compensate for the withdrawal of airframes for this work, squadron aircraft strength was increased by 50%. January brought further success, and on 20 January nine German fighters and fighter-bombers were brought down during an attack on London by 28 enemy aircraft. Six were credited to 609 Squadron including an Fw 190 at an altitude of 27,000ft and three Bf 109s all at 20,000ft

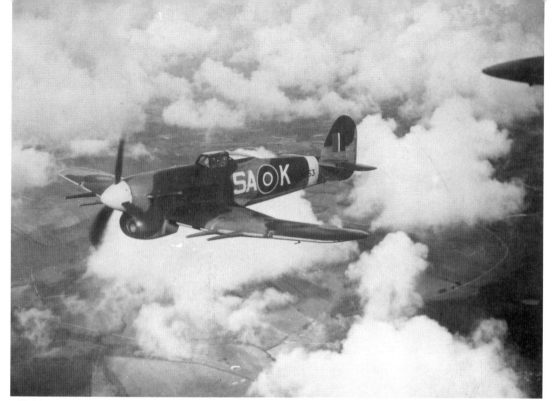

Official Air Ministry photos of JP853/'SA-K' of 486 Squadron. The aircraft joined this unit in October 1943. (Crown Copyright)

JP532/'SA-T', a brand-new 486 Squadron aircraft, photographed in 1943 in one of Tangmere's blast pens. On the left is Fg Off 'Norm' Gall. (Peter Green)

JP504, a new 'OV-Z' for 197 Squadron, seen at Tangmere in October 1943 with Sqn Ldr M C Holmes, Officer Commanding 197 Squadron, in the cockpit. The Squadron Leader's pennant appears on the aircraft's cockpit door. Note the additional small glass 'bubble' on the canopy for the rear-view mirror. (Peter Green)

(the latter all to Fg Off 'Johnny' Baldwin who would become the top air-combat kill pilot on the Typhoon). Enemy attacks also took place over East Anglia.

Although the aircraft's performance was still secret, in its issue for 28 January 1943 *Flight* magazine was able to quote a speed in excess of 400mph (644kph) and that the engine's power rating 'was somewhere around 2,000hp'. 609 Squadron, commanded by Sqn Ldr R P Beamont, was visited by the press in February 1943. At the time 609 Squadron was occupied with 'tip-and-run' raids by Bf 109s and Fw 190s, having downed 16 in the previous three months. In addition, 609 Squadron was performing intruder sorties of its own at night and attacking railway transport in France and Belgium by day. The visit was rounded off by a flying demonstration from Beamont, *Flight* reporting how his performance with the Typhoon 'would have astounded the crowds at a Hendon Display'.

By late April 1943, some 40 tip-and-run raiders had been downed, while on the ground the targets had included goods trains, lorries, barges, tugs and other transport objectives on the roads and rails of France and Belgium. One squadron hit 100 locomotives in just over three months and the Typhoon left its mark over the sea as well, targets such as E-Boats, trawlers and minesweepers having been hit.

On 29 April 1943 two 486 Squadron Typhoons from Tangmere achieved a first for the type when they intercepted a raid from a ground 'scramble', rather than from the usual interceptions by patrols, in the process killing two Bf 109s. On 1 June another five attackers were brought down by 609 Squadron's aircraft during several raids. The pressure had been eased by more effective use of ground radar (the low-level-operating Chain Home Low) which enabled squadrons to hold two aircraft at readiness on their runways with pilots aboard to make instant take-offs when scrambled. Further Typhoon squadrons had moved into the area, and new marks of Griffon-powered Spitfire were also entering service (though at sea level the Typhoon was still about 20mph/32kph faster). However, things suddenly turned much quieter after most of the Typhoon's French-based Luftwaffe opponents were moved to Sicily on 18 June. On 21 October 1943 an Fw 190 was shot down off Beachy Head which, along with three kills in spring 1944, proved to be the last victories by Typhoons in their UK air-defence role.

Offensive Operations from the UK

As the Typhoon became further established there was a gradual switch from air defence to attacks on ground and sea targets – the Typhoon's own 'Rhubarb' operations, although the RAF used separate codenames for different types of attack. A 'Roadstead' was a low-level attack on shipping, a 'Ranger' was a freelance fighter sweep, and an 'Intruder' a 'Rhubarb' made at night.

Five dedicated 'Bombphoon' squadrons were established between September 1942 and May 1943 – 181, 182, 183, 3 and 175 in that order. Having begun with a 250lb (113kg) bomb beneath each wing, the aircraft would eventually carry two 500lb (227kg) or 1,000lb (454kg) bombs for ground-attack work. Although in the early stages often escorted by fighter Typhoons, once they had delivered

Another 182 Squadron Typhoon, 'XM-O', undergoes maintenance. (Peter Green)

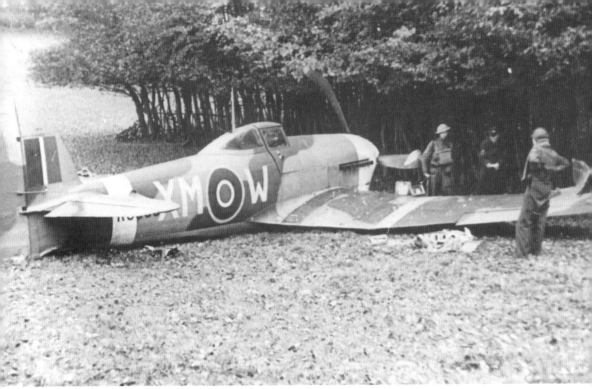

A 182 Squadron aircraft, R8966, seen after suffering a belly landing. (Peter Green)

their loads the bombers themselves still had near full performance (eventually all new Typhoons were equipped to carry bombs). The cannon and bombs weaponry was particularly effective against shipping along the Dutch, Belgian and French coasts.

181 Squadron's story is typical of the 'Tiffy Bomber' units. Once again the early examples suffered from development problems, but 181 Squadron was used to counter attacks by enemy fighter-bombers on British coastal towns before, in February 1943, switching to offensive sweeps, initially against coastal targets but graduating to land targets in northern France. The unit joined the Second Tactical Air Force on its formation in 1943 and operated from southern England. In 1944 it performed ground-attack operations during preparations for the D-Day landings. It moved to France just two weeks after D-Day and was heavily involved in operations to destroy armour during the German retreat from the battle area. The squadron spent the winter based in the Low Countries before moving into Germany for the final offensive, reaching Lübeck by the end of the fighting.

Commanded by Sqn Ldr Dennis Crowley-Milling, 181 Squadron began its Typhoon operational career on 10 February 1943 when (according to *Flight* magazine) four aircraft attacked an armed trawler off the Dutch coast; the vessel was left with a pronounced list and 'had smoke and steam belching from it'. The first attacks over land followed on 22 March with raids over the dispersal points of Alkmaar airfield in Holland, and during the following month the range of targets was expanded to take in harbours and docks, railways and factories, including the bombing of a steelworks in Caen. A nicely timed and particularly successful attack took place on 13 May 1943 on Abbeville airfield when the unit's Typhoons, escorted by Spitfires, discovered a number of Fw 190s refuelling after they had intercepted a raid by US heavy bombers. The enemy aircraft were grouped nicely around their petrol bowsers and presented almost perfect targets.

Four aircraft was the usual number to work as a section and in many mid-1943 sorties 181 Squadron flew two sections of four aircraft with a covering escort of Spitfire IXs. Two groups of four had been found to be the most practical attacking force and having the Spitfires along enabled the Typhoons to concentrate purely on bombing. If the enemy was known to be using radar then the Typhoons would make their approach at ground level before starting a final sharp climb to the required height over the

Aircraft from 181 Squadron are 'bombed up' in readiness for another operation. In fact these views were taken during another Typhoon press day, at Tangmere on 28 June 1943. (Peter Green)

target and peeling off out of the sun to dive down at about a 60° or 70° angle to attack their targets. No airbrakes were fitted, and the flaps were not lowered during the dive.

In July 1943 the RAF formed new Typhoon Wings with 174, 175 and 245 Squadrons at Lydd and 181, 182 and 247 Squadrons at New Romney. On 24 October the 10,000-ton freighter *Münsterland,* loaded with rubber and special metals, was attacked in Cherbourg Harbour by 183 Squadron Typhoons and by Westland Whirlwind fighters of 263 Squadron, with cover from 257 Squadron Typhoons. The heavy defences around Cherbourg accounted for two Whirlwinds (with two more crash-landing) and later, when 183 Squadron attacked separately at 'below mast height', three Typhoons. However, *Münsterland* was hit twice and her progress to Germany was delayed. The ship was attacked once more in early January 1944 at Boulogne by 198 Squadron Typhoons, and was finally sunk on the 20 January by Dover's long-range guns, Typhoons hitting the ship again as it went down.

Overland and coastal operations were fraught with danger, primarily from enemy flak (anti-aircraft gunfire) which took a heavy toll on Typhoons rather than attacks by defending Luftwaffe fighters, although on occasion the latter did make their kill of Typhoons. The British aircraft also added to its list of aerial victories with 14 shot down over Europe before the end of October 1943. In August 1943 45 gal (205l) drop tanks became available which extended the Typhoon's range from 610 miles (982km) to 980 miles (1,577km). To counter flak the Typhoons flew as low as possible, but this meant that if one was hit then the pilot had a much smaller chance of escaping safely.

On two occasions force-landed Typhoons (serials EJ956 in March 1943 and JP548 in February 1944) were made airworthy by the Germans, which enabled them to test-fly Hawker's fighter-bomber at Rechlin, the Luftwaffe's test airfield in eastern Germany. Both of them used Luftwaffe call sign T9+GK and were subsequently lost in crashes, in August and July 1944 respectively.

Returning to 181 Squadron, now in the hands of Sqn Ldr Frank Jensen, on 25 October 1943, as part of a combined operation with five other Typhoon units, it attacked Caen power station using rocket projectiles. Three aircraft were lost but this was the first time that this new weapon had been used in anger.

609 Squadron on 14 May 1943. Flg Off Van Lierde, in DN547 PR-S, prepares to carry out one of the first Typhoon bomber sorties. The 250lb (113kg) bomb is covered in 'Wings for Victory' stamps purchased by station personnel. (Peter Green)

R7752/'PR-G' from 609 Squadron; the mount during the second half of 1942 of Sqn Ldr Paul Richey.

R8830/'EL-U', on loan to A&AEE from 181 Squadron, pictured on a test flight with 500lb (227kg) bombs. (Peter Green)

Underside view of R8830 again. The identity stripes show evidence of recent repairs, possibly due the nature of the trials which were to investigate bomb ricochets during low-level attacks. The cannons have been removed, leaving just the fairings protruding from the wings.

Flg Off C. T. Stimpson of 56 Squadron poses with his Typhoon, EK183/'US-A', at Matlask on 21 April 1943.

By November only 198 and 609 Squadrons remained on low-level fighter defence duties, all of the other Typhoon units having switched to the fighter-bomber role. On 30 November aircraft from 198 Squadron shot down four Fw 190s and hit another while taxiing as three groups of these aircraft were landing at Deelen airfield in Holland.

Towards the end of 1943 the Typhoons found themselves providing some support for the air offensive over Germany. For example, on 30 November and 1 December US bombers supported by fighters attacked Solingen in western Germany and on the first day Spitfires and Typhoons were used to cover the withdrawing bombers, shooting down six enemy aircraft in the process. During the second day of operations the Typhoons together with de Havilland Mosquitos went after enemy shipping around the Brest peninsula. Also in December 1943 the target list began to include the construction sites in the Pas-de-Calais region for launching V-1 flying bombs (codenamed 'Noballs'); the attacks on these sites lasted until July 1944 when the Germans switched to small camouflaged launch sites. These very intensive sorties dominated many of the Typhoon's operations during this period, although enemy fighters, bombers and some transports were also shot down. On 4 December 1943 fighter Typhoons from 198 and 609 Squadrons based at Manston, flying over Holland to support USAAF bomber operations, came across two batches of Dornier Do 217 bombers and claimed 10 destroyed.

By early 1944, with the Sabre engine problems pretty well cured, the first Typhoons with sliding hoods began to arrive. More aircraft were being produced, which allowed further squadrons to equip with the type, and more aircraft carried rockets (as yet there was no specialisation between rocket- and bomb-carrying aircraft). The Typhoon had matured into an extremely capable fighting machine, but by the spring a few units were having their Typhoons replaced by the new Hawker Tempest Mk V; 3 Squadron for example flew its last Typhoon sortie on 24 March 1944.

In January 1944 Typhoons secured 44 aerial victories (on 21 January 198's Fg Off Geoff Eagle downed three Bf 109Gs on his own) and another 20 in February with eight more on the ground;

Typhoon MN192 fresh off the production line at Hucclecote in January 1944. As 'TP-H' of 198 Squadron MN192 was the mount of the Unit's CO, Sqn Ldr J Niblett, who was killed when this aircraft was shot down over Dieppe on 2 June 1944 while making a rocket attack on a radar station. (Peter Green)

Typhoon losses in this period were 34 (just three to enemy aircraft) in January and nearly 40 in February, with the loss of some very experienced pilots. Substantial air-to-air combat on 30 January saw 609 Squadron claim three Fw 190s shot down plus two Ju 88s destroyed on the ground, while in a major battle with Fw 190s from Luftwaffe unit Jagdgeschwader 2 (JG 2) no fewer than nine German fighters were brought down. March was quieter with 31 Typhoons lost against a number of enemy kills, and April even more so as the units began weapons training in readiness for the forthcoming invasion of Europe. However, on 24 April 1944, 438 Squadron's Typhoons dropped 1,000lb (454kg) bombs against a bridge at St-Sauveur, the first occasion this heavier weapon had been taken into action by the aircraft. The 1,000-pounder proved to be particularly effective against bridges.

May brought a huge increase in activity as ground targets were hit to 'prepare' northern France for the invasion. At the start the effort was directed mainly against railway- and river-network targets (bridges, marshalling yards, etc), but from 10 May 1944 the coastal radar system became the Typhoon's prime objective since the type was the most suited to hit these small and difficult targets. Sadly, due to the heavy ground defences around the radar sites, losses were heavy and included many experienced commanders and formation leaders. Over just a few days rocket-armed Typhoons made nearly 700 sorties and it was found that cannon fire was very effective against unprotected control rooms, while the rockets were ideal for the radar scanners and arrays. To help conceal the identity of the Normandy landing sites only one target near to the landing areas was attacked in addition to two further along the coast.

During mid-May 1944 1320 Flight at Holmsley conducted service trials for a new radar-homing device called 'Abdullah', using three Typhoons (MN236, MN263 and MN296) fitted with this equipment. It worked well, but when German radar operators became aware that these aircraft were approaching their stations they would immediately stop any transmissions, so its value was limited. In all, 53 Typhoons were lost during May but the radar campaign was a key success, leaving large portions of the French coast along the Channel without radar cover prior to the landings.

Reconnaissance became another task. From late summer 1944 aircraft were converted for fighter reconnaissance (later called tactical photographic reconnaissance) with a variety of wing-camera fittings replacing one or more of the guns. After trials with JR333, around 120 Typhoons were converted by the RAF itself from May onwards as the FR Mk IB (if armoured), PR Mk IB (no armour) or Tac R Mk IB. The first recipient was 268 Squadron at Odiham with examples arriving from 2 July 1944 onwards, and it made its first recce sorties, over Normandy, on 8 August. 268 Squadron was an independent unit, it did not form part of a Typhoon strike wing and when making photo runs its aircraft would fly at heights between zero and 5,000ft. The objective here was to get the photos home so, when enemy fighters were expected, Typhoons would be used rather than other reconnaissance types, since the 'Tiffy's higher speed provided the best chance of escape. Flak was also a problem but no 268 Squadron Typhoon was lost during the period the unit had the type on strength. During the Falaise battles (see next chapter) they were used to provide intelligence for Supreme Command. 268 Squadron's last Typhoon sortie was made on 19 November 1944.

There was no Operational Training Unit (OTU) for Typhoons until 1944, such was the need to hold aircraft for frontline units, and that meant pilots could not fly the type until they joined an operational squadron. This weakness was finally addressed in April 1944 when 3 Tactical Exercise Unit (TEU) acquired Typhoons in sufficient numbers to provide conversion courses for pilots who had trained on the Hurricane or had flown other types in frontline squadrons. Only in 1945 did full OTUs become available and one of these, 56 OTU, was to be the last unit to operate the Typhoon, keeping examples flying until February 1946.

Above and below: Images showing EK183/'US-A' of 56 Squadron at the Matlask press day on 21 April 1943. The guns are now fully enclosed, whereas previously early Typhoons had their outer barrels exposed. (Peter Green)

Air-to-air shot of EK183/'US-A'.

SW404/'F3-R' of 438 Squadron showing (in silhouette) the rarely seen tropical air-cleaner fitted to production Typhoons from September 1944. This can be seen under the fuselage immediately aft of the radiator fairing. (Chris Thomas)

Typical scene at a Typhoon base in England before the action had moved to Europe. The relatively early aircraft on the left has a three-blade propeller. EK288 sits on the right.

193 Squadron Typhoons lined up on a rather wet runway at Harrowbeer in October 1943. JP919 nearest was one of nine examples presented to the Squadron by the Bellows of Brazil.

The background has been removed by the censor in this shot of a 56 Squadron Typhoon being towed by the unit's tractor on 21 April 1943. (Peter Green)

The port wing underside of a Typhoon FR Mk IB showing the inboard cannon replaced by apertures for three photo-reconnaissance cameras.

A 609 Squadron scene at Manston in April 1943 with Sqn Ldr Beamont's 'PR-G' (with yellow cannon barrels) circling overhead. (Peter Green)

EK139/'HH-N' of 175 Squadron is armed with dummy bombs for training purposes in May 1944. (Peter Green)

EJ922/'QO-F' of 3 Squadron in the summer of 1943. (Peter Green)

198 Squadron Typhoon JR371/'TP-R' was photographed at Manston in January 1944 fitted with long-range tanks. (Peter Green)

Chapter 5

Typhoon Operations: Europe

In March 1944 Exercise 'Spartan' was held in southern England to help prepare RAF units for the invasion of Europe and the Typhoon squadrons that took part were 181, 182, 183 and 247, the programme including operating from mobile airfields and living under canvas (which would become the norm later in the year). The Second Tactical Air Force or 2TAF was formed from within Fighter Command on 13 November 1943, as an element of the Allied Expeditionary Air Force to support the D-Day landings and the invasion. 2TAF took over light-bomber units from Bomber Command and various squadrons from Fighter Command. The Typhoon units were split into 83 and 84 Groups while those fighter squadrons retained for UK home defence became 'The Air Defence of Great Britain' (ADGB reverted to the title Fighter Command in October 1944). The Typhoon units assigned to 2TAF put in spells at Armament Practice Camp to prepare them for their dedicated roles, either rocket-firing or dive-bombing.

On 4 June 1944 all Typhoons were given 'Invasion Stripes'. On D-Day itself, 6 June, 20 squadrons were on call for 2TAF, nine of which would operate in 'Air Alert' duties with the three Canadian squadrons of 143 Wing (438, 439 and 440) becoming the first over the beaches. The other units dealt with targets further inland as in previous days. The first Typhoons to land on a French base, or rather a hastily prepared landing strip with wire-mesh runway built with 'Sommerfield tracking', was a

A sight to bring terror to German ground forces – nose-on view of a Hawker Typhoon in a dive.

Relatively poor-quality picture showing JP380/'XM-Y' of 182 Squadron at New Romney in October 1943. Petrol cans are piled up in the foreground. (Peter Green)

damaged 245 Squadron aircraft on the 10 June. On the 13 June 1944, however, examples began using the new strips to land and rearm and refuel during the day, but would then return to their main bases in England at night. The support operations included attacks on several German HQs, which resulted in the deaths of two Generals and other officers.

Based Overseas

The new improvised and temporary airfields were known as Advanced Landing Grounds or ALGs and were created specifically for the tactical air forces to support the advancing ground armies engaged on the battlefield. As the front line moved further forward and gradually out of range for the Typhoons, new ALGs were built closer to the action to which the aircraft then transferred. Those ALGs left in the rear were either used for support roles or abandoned. The ALGs and the equipment and materials required to construct them was just one element of the vast and complex preparations and plans undertaken prior to the invasion.

Aircraft based at the first of these new strips (B.2, B.3 and B.6 with 'B' for British – 'A' was allocated for American strips) were parked within just a few miles of the front line and were thus exposed to enemy shellfire, and at one stage from the 22 June the Typhoons had to return to English soil. Back at home another problem had to be dealt with. The fine soil in France, exposed during the construction of the new landing strips, created dust storms when the aircraft took off, and in just a few days of operations the soil particles that had been sucked into the engine had resulted in excessive wear to the Sabre's sleeve valves; the rate of attrition was so serious that it began to affect the air offensive.

Flt Off Hank Nixon RCAF about to taxi in his 137 Squadron Typhoon at Helmond in March 1945. The ground crew standing by far left holds a fire extinguisher, standard practice on start-up. Note the metal 'taxiway'. (Chris Thomas)

Wg Cdr Charles Green in his Typhoon MN666, 121 Wing, Holmsley South in June 1944. (Chris Thomas)

The back of this photo suggests that this might be a large group of Typhoons going into battle during the break-out from the Normandy beach head. In truth this extraordinary formation was photographed in Germany in the summer of 1945 when a number of flypasts were arranged for celebrations.

The problems of operating from advanced landing strips in Normandy are shown graphically by the clouds of dust thrown up by this 198 Squadron Typhoon. (Peter Green)

Typhoons from 137 Squadron taxi and take-off from Eindhoven in about October 1944. (Fg Off Ken Brain DFC via Peter Green)

After a request for help the Napier Flight Development Establishment at Luton, in the form of Cecil Cowdrey (General Manager of Napier) and a Mr Bonar, designed, built and test-flew in just ten hours what they called the Momentum Type air filter. This provided a filtering capacity of 96%, which immediately prolonged the engine's life many times over without affecting the power output in any serious way. The filter operated on the deflection principle, Cowdrey and Bonar having produced a mushroom-shaped dome to go over the carburettor air intake which deflected the worst of the dust away but permitted the air to enter behind. Produced in Luton in large numbers, this stop-gap was subsequently replaced by a drum-shaped filter which was also fitted with 'cuckoo-doors', the latter to cope with the fact that the Typhoon engine would on occasion backfire.

After their return to Normandy it was also realised that the invasion stripes made the Typhoons on the ground visible to enemy aircraft flying above, so those on the upper surfaces and fuselage sides were removed. By September some examples only had the stripes beneath the rear fuselage remaining.

By the end of June all of 83 Group's Typhoons were based in France, and those from 84 Group had begun to join them. But in the days since 6 June well over 60 Typhoons had been lost, mostly to flak with just six falling to enemy aircraft. On the 29 June five Bf 109s were claimed as shot down during a battle with 193 Squadron's Typhoons. In the meantime 137 and 263 Squadrons, held back as part of ADGB (the latter a 'double' squadron since it flew one flight with bomber Typhoons and the other with rocket aircraft), suffered losses attacking shipping in the Channel.

From 22 June 137 Squadron began interception sorties against the V-1 flying bombs that were now being launched against southern England, shooting down 30 during the summer period. One was brought down using a standard rocket projectile, while another was downed using special rockets fitted

Fully armed MN234 of 137 Squadron at Eindhoven, October 1944. (Fg Off Ken Brain DFC via Peter Green)

'SF-R' of 137 Squadron, PD611, pictured in 1944. Note that the D-Day stripes have been removed from the upper fuselage and from the upper and lower surfaces of the wings. (Fg Off Ken Brain DFC via Peter Green)

Gp Capt D J Scott who led an attack on a gun position at Le Havre. The photo is dated September 1944.

MN995/'SF-X' of 137 Squadron trails an undercarriage leg. Another photo taken at Eindhoven in about October 1944. (Fg Off Ken Brain DFC via Peter Green)

The sequence of Eindhoven 137 Squadron pictures ends with a side view of 'SF-K'. Another Typhoon flies overhead. (Fg Off Ken Brain DFC via Peter Green)

with 25lb (11kg) warheads and a photoelectric cell inside a Bakelite head, which would be triggered if it passed very close to a flying bomb. In addition, the French-based Typhoons began to attack the V-1s at their launch sites. In all, fewer than 60 Typhoons were lost during July.

The next job for the Typhoon was interdiction, the hitting of targets just behind the enemy's front-line as a direct support for the Allied armies and to prevent the build-up of reinforcements. It was during this period that the 'cab-rank' system came into operation, aircraft on patrol being directed by a Visual Control Post (usually an armoured vehicle) to hit targets very close to the front when required, and at very short notice. This was to prove crucial in the next stage of the Battle of Normandy, the few days in the campaign that would give the Typhoon its two great moments in history.

Mortain and Falaise

On 7 August 1944, the German 57th Panzer Korps launched Operation Luettich, a major counter-attack in the region around Mortain, which raised the possibility that the American Third Army might be cut off by a thrust to the sea, thus preventing a breakout from Normandy. However, as the situation developed the German armour was allowed to fall into a trap. It was agreed that the USAAF should attack the enemy's supply lines and also provide a defensive fighter screen (Allied air superiority during this day proved crucial), leaving the Typhoon's of 121 Wing to concentrate on the Panzers. Early morning mist prevented any air operations until late morning, but when 174 Squadron, operating from airfield B.5 and 181 from B.6, waded into the enemy in the early afternoon, they found a long column of 260 tanks and vehicles stretching along a main road between St-Barthelemy and Cherence.

Hitting the front and back ends first to block the enemy's escape, these and further Typhoon squadrons then operated a 'shuttle-service' to destroy all of the vehicles trapped in between. With little organised flak, and with the American fighters blocking out the Luftwaffe entirely, Typhoon losses were very light. A total of 294 Typhoon sorties were flown at Mortain during an 8½ hour period, 80 tons of bombs and 2,088 rockets were delivered to a hapless enemy and, with the help of US ground forces, the German advance was halted. Other Typhoons flew operations against another Panzer attack at Vire.

The halting of the German counter-attack meant that the Allies could now break out. As the Germans retreated, the Allied ground forces closed around the enemy's 7th Army and trapped it within the narrow lanes near Falaise, RAF Bomber Command having raided the town itself to make it impassable. With only a small gap left at Chambois, on 18 August the Typhoons attacked the retreating ground forces in strength and the result was the most ghastly carnage and huge losses. By late afternoon vast numbers of German vehicles had become jammed outside Vimoutiers and the Typhoons of 83 Group wrought havoc. This time the defensive fire was very heavy and 17 Typhoons were brought down on the 18 August, with another 11 the following day (in all, 90 were lost during August). Once again, however, the Luftwaffe's fighters were able to break through to the Typhoons on just two occasions, almost always being thrown back by the USAAF, though on the 17 August four Typhoons were shot down when 183 Squadron was hit by Bf 109s. The fighting lasted until 25 August and the enemy vehicles that did escape were harried again further along their line of retreat, at bottlenecks such as at Orlec.

On 12 October 1944 *Flight* published an interview with Wg Cdr W Dring, Wing Commander Operations of 123 Typhoon Wing. He reported how 'the Typhoons queued up and waited for the German transport to cross the bomb line', while on another occasion they demolished two houses specifically to block a road, and then waited for the transport to build up behind this road block. 'Such was the accuracy of the rocket-firing' Dring declared, that the Typhoons were using the weapon almost as super-artillery and it could destroy pillboxes and guns. It was claimed that the 'cab rank' system, with pilots directed by radio to specific targets by an observer at a Visual Control Point, enabled the fighter-bombers to deal with targets within 200 yards of Allied troops, at the time one of the closest forms of air support yet devised. At this stage 123 Wing had, since D-Day (according to Dring), destroyed 94 enemy tanks while leaving another 70 emitting smoke, plus 352 transport vehicles left in flames with another 400 smoking (figures quoted in *Flight*).

The capability of the Typhoon's rocket armament has over the years grown to almost mythical proportions, when it was nothing like the precision anti-tank weapon for which it has so often been given credit; it was the Typhoon's cannon that proved more effective in destroying transport and supply vehicles and German light half-tracks. The truth is that the unguided rocket-projectile was a crude weapon formed from a 3in-diameter (7.6cm) cast-iron pipe with four cruciform stabilising fins attached to the rear end. A cordite rocket motor went inside the tube and there was a 25lb (11kg) armour-piercing head for dealing with armoured vehicles or a 60lb (27kg) semi-armour-piercing head for ships, the latter with 17lb (7.7kg) of high-explosive inside. Trials showed that the two forms worked best the other way around – the solid shot version was better suited for ships and U-boats because it remained stable underwater, while the explosive version proved effective against armour. The latter altogether weighed 91lb (41kg) and after launching could accelerate to a speed of around 1,600ft/sec in just 500 yards/457m (this was of course on top of the speed at which the aircraft carrying it was flying). Once the motor had burnt out the rocket would gradually slow down and coast to its target.

Methods devised by Typhoon pilots for rockets attacks were as follows:

1. Heavily defended targets: dive at a 60° angle from around 8,000ft, fire all eight rockets as a salvo at around 4,000ft, pull up into a zoom climb to avoid flak batteries. With the angle, this meant that the rockets had to travel about 1,700 yards to reach their objective.
2. Lightly defended targets: dive at 25° from 3,500ft, then fire rockets in pairs at around 1,500ft. When fired here the weapons were about 1,000 yards from their target.

All of this had to be done 'by eye', so there was little margin for error, particularly as the rear fins could also make the rocket 'weathercock' – ie, veer in the direction of the airflow, important if the Typhoon was pulling 'G' at the moment of release.

Dr Alfred Price analysed the performance of the rocket projectile in an RAF Historical Society paper (*The Rocket-Firing Typhoons in Normandy*). At Mortain 84 tanks were claimed destroyed by the Typhoons, but a close examination of the battle area after the Germans had departed showed just 43 left behind, with only seven destroyed by air-launched rockets and two by bombs (and 19 by ground anti-tank weapons). The difference was in part due to the confusion of the battle, smoke, some tanks were attacked more than once, etc, and that some damaged vehicles may have been removed by the Germans. At the Falaise Gap it was calculated that just 14 tanks were destroyed by rockets, four by bombs, with 21 lightly armoured vehicles destroyed by cannon or machine-gun fire. A very large number were abandoned by their crews, often because they were hemmed in by the tactic of hitting the front and back of convoys first, or because they were out of fuel. For other vehicles (supply lorries, etc) rockets claimed six, bombs 52 and guns no fewer than 377, and it was the destruction of so many supply vehicles that created a shortage of fuel.

This is not an attempt to devalue the work and achievements of the Typhoon, which were phenomenal, but to highlight how a myth has grown around the rocket projectile. At Mortain and Falaise the Typhoon and its rockets did leave their mark, most of all on the morale of crews who abandoned their tanks and ran for cover. Until Mortain on 7 August German armour had not appeared in force in the open in Normandy during daylight hours. Although the rockets were nothing like as accurate as first credited, if one did hit a tank directly then it would destroy it. However, a miss by only

This Mk IB, SW406 from the last production batch, carries code 'ZH' which identifies it as belonging to 266 Squadron.

10–12ft (3.0–3.7m) would do little damage and if the pilot missed the point-of-fire limits listed above by just a small margin, the rocket could miss its target by a long way. Nevertheless, the successes at Mortain and Falaise could and would not have been so quick and so complete without the Typhoon, and in the eyes of the Germans these events took the rocket-firing Typhoon's reputation to an even higher level. It was a reputation that was fully deserved! In excess of 220,000 rocket projectiles were fired during the European war and the vast majority were delivered by Typhoons.

Tragically, there were incidents of 'friendly fire' when Typhoons attacked Allied forces. The worst case was a raid by 263 and 266 Squadrons on 27 August against four 'enemy' minesweepers and some trawlers off Cap d'Antifer, Le Havre. These were actually Royal Navy vessels, two minesweepers (HMS *Britomart* and *Hussar*) took direct hits and were sunk, another (HMS *Salamander*) was so badly damaged with its stern blown off that she was written off as a constructive total loss, and most of the other ships were damaged to some degree; the loss of life was considerable. Here the ferocious effect of Typhoon weaponry was seen at first-hand by the British, while the lack of information provided for this minesweeping operation highlighted an appalling error in communications.

After Mortain and Falaise, the Typhoons worked next on stopping the remains of the German 7th Army from getting across the Seine, the last permanent bridge over the river being eventually destroyed by Typhoons. Germany's withdrawal from France was rapid and British forces began a rush towards Belgium, the Typhoon units having to move quickly to keep up. 146 Wing's aircraft had to return to Manston for a period to enable them to continue raiding the retreating Germans in northern France and Belgium. By mid-September the British had progressed into Holland and on 17 October Operation *Market Garden* began with the British 1st Airborne Division dropping into Arnhem, Typhoons having hit defensive guns around the town before the parachute drops could start. British armour was to move forward and link up with the Arnhem forces using 'cab-rank' Typhoons to help clear the way. Unfortunately, the weather deteriorated and after 18 October the RAF was unable to give much support. *Market Garden* was abandoned on 25 October and the remaining British forces were evacuated.

By the end of September 124 and 143 Wing Typhoons were based at B.78 airfield at Eindhoven while the Squadrons forming 121 Wing had gone to B.80 at Volkel (since D-Day the compositions of the Wings had changed through various squadron movements). These three Wings would continue to support the Army as it moved towards Germany, but 123 and 146 Wings now concentrated on hitting German garrisons in ports and other bases by-passed in the Allied charge. These included German forces on Walcheren Island and in the estuary of the River Scheldt, their presence still preventing the use of the port of Antwerp. Also, by late September Typhoons were operating over Germany itself.

Final Stages

For a period the Allied advance came to a halt and the Typhoons concentrated on interdiction sorties behind enemy lines against railway and road targets such as bridges, in part to prevent the supply of equipment to the V-1 flying bomb and V-2 rocket launching sites. Other targets were German SS and Army headquarters. With operations over a wider area Typhoon losses for the three-month period September to November 1944 dropped to 108, with very few falling to enemy aircraft. The severe winter weather of December slowed everything down and, since so few bases had hangers, it made operating Typhoons in the open a miserable job for the groundcrews.

Things changed on the 17 December when the Germans launched a counter offensive in the Ardennes – The Battle of the Bulge. For seven days Allied ground forces had to defend themselves without air cover, the overcast weather being so poor, but from the 24 December 1944 it improved and the Typhoons returned, although quite a number were shot down on this day by enemy fighters. At least 10 Typhoons were lost in air-to-air fighting in December and another 37 fell to other causes during the offensive, but the enemy's progress was halted.

The aftermath of Operation Bödenplatte – the remains of 439 Squadron RCAF Typhoons at Eindhoven on 1 January 1945 after enemy air attacks. (Peter Green)

On 1 January 1945 Operation *Bödenplatte* began; a Luftwaffe attempt to cripple the Allied Air Forces in the region using massed attacks by swarms of Fw 190s and Bf 109s. Seventeen air bases were raided without warning including three occupied by Typhoons – Deurne (three Typhoons damaged with some Spitfires destroyed), Eindhoven (20 Typhoons destroyed by JG 3 – some as they were taking off – and another 14 damaged) and Volkel (Typhoons not touched). At Eindhoven 440 Squadron was left with just four serviceable Typhoons and overall a large number of Allied aircraft were destroyed during these raids, but the enemy's losses were heavy and could not be replaced. Most of the Allied aircraft were unoccupied and the Typhoon units for example had new aircraft within a few days, their pilots returning to Britain to collect and ferry them back to Belgium. Gloster Aircraft's ability to keep delivering new Typhoons throughout the conflict needs to be mentioned here, although rebuilt airframes also bolstered the supply.

In the short term *Bödenplatte* was a success for the Luftwaffe, but long term, a failure and a disaster since so many experienced pilots were lost. From this point the Luftwaffe was no longer an effective fighting force and the Allies could claim air superiority. During the air combats that day 439 Squadron claimed four Fw 190s shot down for the loss of one Typhoon.

Following another lull due to bad weather, February brought a return to ground-attack operations. As the Allies moved towards the Rhine under Operation *Veritable* the Typhoons returned to their 'cab-rank' technique to destroy more armour and vehicles than at any time since Falaise, in addition to hitting other defensive positions. Two of the new Messerschmitt Me 262 jet fighters were downed by 439 Squadron on 14 February 1945.

A 164 Squadron Mk IB photographed (it is thought) in 1945. Note the underwing tanks and four-blade propeller.

In March, after the Allies had reached the Rhine, attacks on Army HQs and interdiction operations against road, rail and river facilities and traffic, including barges, were made to help pave the way for the next stage of the advance. Here, a few missions employed a blind bombing technique. Three days prior to the crossing of the Rhine, on 24 March 121 Wing's Typhoons moved to a new base at Goch, B.100, which was the first British airfield set up within Germany itself. For this next advance the Typhoons went flat-out dealing with flak defences (to prevent glider-towing and parachute aircraft from being shot down) or on the usual 'cab-rank' duties. Once again the type's contribution proved vital and only six troop-carrying aircraft were shot down by flak.

In the meantime, in part to counter a shortage of pilots, one Typhoon squadron per wing was disbanded (168, 257 and 174) between late February and early April 1945. Also during January the invasion stripes finally disappeared and other changes were made to the aircraft's markings (such as white rings around the upper wing roundels) to try to prevent attacks by Allied fighters. However, such was the type's similarity to the Fw 190 that the odd Typhoon was still downed or damaged by friendly fire, and in both February and March over 40 Typhoons were lost on operations. It must be pointed out, however, that many pilots were able to bale out and the Typhoon (and the Tempest which followed) gained a reputation, thanks to the heavy airframe and large engine, for protecting its pilots in crash-landings. For the same reasons many more aircraft still got home despite suffering substantial damage.

As the advance beyond the Rhine moved forward, 123 Wing's Typhoons were used to help finish the enemy resistance in Arnhem. Others attacked German airfields while forces trying to escape to Norway across the Baltic were also targeted. On 4 April two Typhoons from 438 Squadron were shot down

DN248 of 245 Squadron at Westhampnett sits quietly under a heated cover in December 1943 or January 1944, while groundcrew queue at a NAAFI mobile canteen. (Peter Green)

SW494/'EL-F' of 181 Squadron viewed just after taking off from Helmond on 26 March 1945. (Public Archives of Canada via Peter Green)

A 257 Squadron Typhoon pictured during the freezing winter of 1944/45. (Peter Green)

by Bf 109s, the final examples to fall victim to enemy aircraft. On the 26 April an Me 262 was shot down by 263 Squadron, the last enemy fighter to succumb to a Typhoon, but in early May examples of the Blohm & Voss Bv 138, Ha 139 and Bv 222 flying boats were destroyed. As enemy forces tried to escape north great numbers of road vehicles and trains were despatched, but the sinking of the liner *Cap Arcona* proved to be tragic since this was being used as a floating prison ship. In all, 45 Typhoons were lost during April and the first four days of May 1945. The German armies then surrendered and the air fighting came to an abrupt end.

The subsequent disbandment or re-equipping of Typhoon units was swift with the first, 164 Squadron, returning to England in May to receive Spitfires; other units would soon upgrade to the Tempest Mk II. Those Typhoons still in Germany concentrated on training but did get the chance to do some display flying and flag-waving. Redundant Typhoons were retired, the oldest and most worn out being scrapped, but those in the best condition were flown into store at 5, 20 and 51 Maintenance Units. In the process 83 and 84 Group Support Units became 83 and 84 Group Disbandment Centres to help with the process of winding down the Typhoon organisation. 247 Squadron flew some Typhoons in the Battle of Britain flypast held over London on 15 September 1945, but by the end of that month all Typhoon units based in Germany had disbanded. The stored airframes did not last long, mostly going for scrap in 1947, although a few ground-instruction airframes lasted until 1955. Of the 3,316 Typhoons built only one complete example still exists, MN325 at the RAF Museum, Hendon.

137 Squadron aircraft with anti-personnel RP under the port wing and the usual semi-armour piercing/high explosive (SAP/HE) RP under the starboard wing, Helmond, March 1945. This ensured that when a pair of rockets was fired it comprised one of each. (Chris Thomas)

Mishap at 56 OTU in August 1945 with Mk IBs piled up. The pilot of Typhoon 'HQ-E' at the back lost control on landing and ran into some parked aircraft. (Peter Green)

Typhoon SW532, formerly of 245 Squadron, is seen stored at 51 Maintenance Unit at Lichfield in 1946.

In Conclusion

In 1939 one of Germany's most important aircraft was the Junkers Ju 87 dive-bomber, the famous Stuka, which was successful in helping its nation's armed forces spread their way across neighbouring countries. The Battle of Britain, however, revealed how vulnerable the Ju 87 was to fighter attack. In many ways, following D-Day the Typhoon performed the same type of role as the Stuka, but it possessed far more powerful armament and had the guns and an engine to allow it to mix with enemy fighters on a near-equal footing. After D-Day the Typhoon was still able to shoot down 50 enemy aircraft and destroy plenty more on the ground.

This text has highlighted how the Hawker Typhoon experienced substantial success as a pure fighter, a fact not acknowledged as often as it should be, before moving on to the role that brought true fame, as a dive-bomber and ground-attack fighter creating havoc over enemy-occupied Europe. The Typhoon's greatest moment has to be its achievements as a rocket-firing close-support fighter at Mortain and Falaise. Having streams of Typhoons on call to hit, break up and destroy the massive concentrations of enemy tanks and armour in Normandy eventually enabled Allied ground forces to break out and advance, steps that eventually brought ultimate victory (but not before more than 500 Typhoons had been lost on operations).

With the end of the war in 1945 and the advance of jet aircraft making Hawker's heavy fighter-bomber pretty well obsolete, the Typhoon's moment in history had passed. The follow-on Tempest would serve the post-war RAF, but by the end of 1945 the Typhoon had all but disappeared from the inventory. It had operated almost exclusively in the UK and in Europe and never fought anywhere else, but that was enough to ensure that the Typhoon would be classed as a great aircraft.

Typhoon RB207/'F3-T' of 438 Squadron taxies through flood water at Eindhoven in February 1945, while another pilot uses a dinghy to reach his aircraft. Just some of the difficulties of operating in the open during spells of inclement winter weather. (Chris Thomas)

Chapter 6

Memories

R egrettably, there are few Typhoon pilots left who can explain first-hand what this extraordinary aeroplane was like to fly. Fortunately the author was able to contact one gentleman whose entire combat flying career was spent on the Typhoon.

Flying Officer Derek E F Tapson

Derek Tapson trained as a pilot in America before completing his advanced training in Scotland on the Hawker Hurricane. He flew Typhoons exclusively with 197 Squadron, performing operations against the advance of German tank forces on D-Day, and then throughout the Normandy invasion. He was shot down on 10 February 1945 and spent the last months of the war as a prisoner of war. On return

Staff and crew of 84 Group Support Unit's Test Flight pictured at Thruxton near Andover in September 1944. The OC was Sqn Ldr Martin. (Derek Tapson)

to the UK he was diagnosed with jaundice and was not permitted to fly in the RAF any more – he even had his log book taken away, which meant there were no accessible records to put dates to some of what follows. Derek became a photographic officer, before leaving the RAF in late 1946. Post-war he did a lot of gliding and became a gliding examiner.

I joined 197 Squadron based at Tangmere in December 1943 and, apart from one short period, served with that unit for the whole of my time on the Typhoon, completing 123 sorties with the aircraft. In fact I never flew any other type on operations and not many other combat types at all (apart from the Hurricane during weapons training). When 197 moved to Normandy in July 1944 it was found that there was insufficient accommodation to take all of the squadron's pilots, so two of us had to stay behind with 84 Group Support Unit's Test Flight at Thruxton. We re-joined 197 when it had moved to Lille and I flew with the Squadron as it worked its way across Europe [197 was at Lille-Vendeville for a short period between 11 September and 2 October 1944].

When I moved on to the Typhoon I found the aircraft astonishing and exciting since it was 100mph faster that the Hurricane, and the extra speed was of course a big advantage. As part of my training I had flown the Hurricane a great deal and so could appreciate the extra power that was available. It was quite easy to fly, the controls were straightforward and I enjoyed flying it very much. I did fly a Spitfire once, just to see what it was like, but I was not that keen (having no logbook means I cannot remember which mark of Spitfire it was). I remember that the view out was not as good as the Typhoon. I never had the chance to fly a Tempest and so cannot make a comparison there.

As a Squadron 197 was split into A and B Flights and each pilot, 12 in all if I remember, had his own aircraft. I cannot remember the serial number for mine [Derek did at one stage fly Mk IB MN925/'OV-Z']. Our normal targets were all on the ground – airfields, railways, troops, anything! The 20mm cannon was very good and very destructive and we never carried the rocket projectiles used by other units, but we did drop loads of bombs up to 1,000lb (454kg) in size [197 Squadron was one of the Typhoon units allocated to bombing only and not rocket-firing]. I never had any trouble or mishaps with the Sabre engine – it was very good, nice and powerful and for example made the climb quite straightforward.

Since we concentrated on ground-attack for almost all of the time we never had much opportunity to do aerobatics, but if required the Typhoon could loop the loop without trouble. We would usually take off in formation in pairs and just concentrate on our next target, which also meant that we never mixed with enemy fighters, although I do remember on one occasion meeting up with a couple of German fighters. However, they flew away towards a town protected by balloons and there was no point in getting involved, so I never had the chance to shoot anything down which was a bit of a disappointment. That said, not being involved in air-to-air combat was an advantage because it meant that our operations were much simpler to plan and carry out. The Typhoon was not so good at high altitude and we never went above 21,000ft; in fact we usually flew to our targets at about 10,000ft.

The day I was shot down we were attacking a building in Northern Germany, just over the Rhine. At the time we were at a base [Mill] just outside Germany and had been there for just a few days. During the operation our CO told us he could not identify the specific building we were to attack, but I was flying as No 2 to my Flight Commander and we were able to identify it and made our diving attack. As we pulled up I moved to the side behind my Flight Commander, a move which I think was very lucky for me because, had I not done so, I think the shell which then hit me would have come into the fuselage or cockpit rather than hitting the engine. I was hit while only at about 2,000ft altitude, but my luck held because I was able to climb to 8,000ft when I could then see our airfield.

However, fire broke out which prevented me from trying for base and I had no choice but to bale out. I jettisoned the canopy and put the stick forward to prevent a spin, but having already released my harness this move made the aircraft throw me out of the cockpit. I was in fact briefly knocked out – I think my head hit the fixed part of the windscreen – and I fell to 1,500ft before releasing my parachute. On landing I was surrounded by German troops but I was well looked after, although my eyebrows had been burned away by the cockpit fire.

I look back on my time with 197 Squadron really just as a job – that was how we approached it – but I made a lot of good friends.

Author's note: Information on 197 Squadron's wartime role and aircrew can be found at an excellent website: 197typhoon.org.uk. In an interview, Sqn Ldr Allan H Smith, 197 CO between July and December 1944, said:

During my time 197 was always a bomber unit undertaking both dive-bombing and low-level attacks. We preferred low-level using bombs with 11-second delay fuses and employed a technique that made it near impossible to miss a building target. Prior to the raid we worked out an approach route that took us in below the height of the building to be hit and would release our bombs at the last possible moment. This would enable the Typhoon to clear the building, while the bombs had nowhere else to go but into the side of the building. The pilots were flying up to four missions a day, usually in a hail of flak, and on many occasions saw their best friends shot down.

Smith was himself shot down by Flak over Holland on 31 December 1944 and became a POW.

Flight

In April 1944 *Flight* magazine published a report that quoted a senior test pilot who had been asked to sample the Typhoon. He noted that the predominant impression for a pilot making his first flight in the type was of incredible power. Naturally on take-off there was a tendency to swing but this was easily corrected, the undercarriage retracted quickly and the aeroplane accelerated rapidly to its best climbing speed. In the air the ease of handling of both aircraft and engine gave great confidence, which quickly countered the 'big machine' feeling any fighter pilot experienced on first entering the cockpit. Indeed, when required the Typhoon was 'very agile and nimble' and all manoeuvres were possible over a wide

Aircraft of 197 Squadron on the airfield at Manston. (Derek Tapson)

range of airspeeds. In addition, both loops and rolls could be performed 'at rates varying from the very slow and graceful to the extremely snappy'. Thanks to the available power and speed, upward rolls and loops could be made to cover 6,000ft of vertical space, which was not only a nice addition to aerobatics but also actually contributed enormously to the Typhoon's ability to fight. With a little flap, steep turns could be made down to a very low airspeed.

In the air the Sabre's 24 cylinders and high rpm gave the pilot 'a pleasant feeling of humming along' but also an impression of substantial power. The Typhoon's thick wing gave 'extraordinary gentle behaviour at the stall', the right wing usually dropping gently in a straight stall, and even in a high-speed stall the machine's behaviour was still good. After the stall the recovery was quick. Since the main undercarriage legs did not come down quite in step, when preparing to land, the aircraft would yaw slightly to one side and then to the other. The flaps were powerful and slowed the Typhoon down quickly, and the landing itself was straightforward. There was no tendency for wing-drop but, thanks to the big elevator, the pilot could often find that he was landing tail first. Making a three-point landing did require a little more judgement than was usual on other types of aircraft.

Aircraft of 197 Squadron pictured just after their move to B.3 St. Croix airfield in Normandy in July 1944. (Derek Tapson)

Typhoons of 197 Squadron at Manston in September 1944. They were based here for a short period because, at the time, there was no suitable airstrip near the front line that was fit for them to use. In the background gliders are prepared for the Arnhem operation. (Derek Tapson)

Typhoons and 'Erks', RAF slang for groundcrew. (Derek Tapson)

The CO of 197 Squadron when it joined 146 Wing of 2TAF was Sqn Ldr D M 'Dutch' Taylor, pictured here with Fg Off Gerry Mahaffy. (Derek Tapson)

At that time 197's Flight Commanders were Flt Lts Ted Jolleys and Jonny Johnson. (Derek Tapson)

A briefing for 197 Squadron prior to another mission. (Derek Tapson)

Arming one of 197's aircraft at around the time of the Falaise action. (Derek Tapson)

Some of the German armour destroyed during the Falaise Pocket battle in mid-August 1944, the decisive engagement in the Battle of Normandy. (Derek Tapson)

One of 197 Squadron's pilots photographed in his Typhoon, aircraft 'Z', which has the name 'The Jones Boys, Murder Inc' painted just ahead of the canopy. (Derek Tapson)

The pilots of B Flight 197 Squadron pose at Derne-Antwerp with Typhoon 'OV-G' in 1944. Sitting left to right on the aircraft itself are Plt Off D I McFee (who in December 1944 became a POW), Fg Off J K 'Paddy' Byrne, Plt Off D E F 'Red' Matthews and Plt Off James, Flt Sgt R B 'Bobby' Farmiloe sits on the nose, and on the other wing are Plt Off D G Lovell, Fg Off K K Welsh RAAF and Plt Off W D 'Jock' Ellis. Standing in front of the aircraft left to right are Flt Lt G G Mahaffy, Sqn Ldr A H Smith RNZAF, and Flt Lt R C Curwen (who from January 1945 took command of the Squadron). It is thought that everyone in the picture survived the war. (Derek Tapson)

Flg Off Johnny Rook's regular mount, RB251/'OV-G', was named 'Brenda IX' and is seen at field B.89 Mil in February 1945 carrying long-tailed 500lb (227kg) bombs. (Chris Thomas)

Chapter 7

Description

The Hawker Typhoon was a single-seat low-wing fighter. Its fuselage had a tubular girder structure at the front, while the rear portion was constructed as a stressed-skin shell with flush riveting. At the front the fuselage had a primary structure of steel and light-alloy tubes covered with sheet-metal panels. The rear fuselage was produced in two parts, the rearmost of which was integral with the multi-spar fin, and the tailplane halves (and elevators) were symmetrical and thus interchangeable for port or starboard fitting. The rudder was the only control surface to have fabric covering. The Typhoon's two-spar light-alloy mainplanes had no centre section and were attached directly to the fuselage primary structure. The metal ailerons were of the modified Frise type and split trailing-edge flaps extended from the ailerons to the fuselage.

A single Napier Sabre 24-cylinder H-type sleeve-valve liquid-cooled two-speed-supercharged piston engine was mounted on the tubular steel frame and drove a three- or four-blade airscrew. The radiator and oil-cooler units were housed in a cowling directly beneath the nose. Compared to many contemporary fighters the Typhoon had a very short nose, a result of the Sabre's cylinder configuration

DN411 (with white nose) pictured at Brockworth in July 1943. One of Gloster's factory buildings is on the right and the A W Hawksley Ltd works are in the background. More Typhoons stand in the left background with Armstrong Whitworth Albemarle bombers both on the right and behind DN411. The aircraft sitting directly behind the Typhoon may be a Miles Master advanced trainer. (Jet Age Museum)

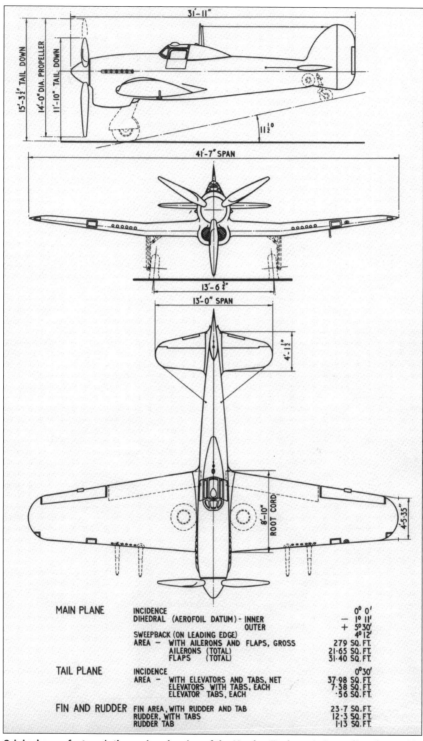

MAIN PLANE	INCIDENCE		0° 0'
	DIHEDRAL (AEROFOIL DATUM) - INNER		− 1° 11'
	OUTER		+ 5° 30'
	SWEEPBACK (ON LEADING EDGE)		4° 12'
	AREA − WITH AILERONS AND FLAPS, GROSS		279 SQ. FT.
	AILERONS (TOTAL)		21·65 SQ. FT.
	FLAPS (TOTAL)		31·40 SQ. FT.
TAIL PLANE	INCIDENCE		0°30'
	AREA − WITH ELEVATORS AND TABS, NET		37·98 SQ. FT.
	ELEVATORS WITH TABS, EACH		7·38 SQ. FT.
	ELEVATOR TABS, EACH		·56 SQ. FT.
FIN AND RUDDER	FIN AREA, WITH RUDDER AND TAB		23·7 SQ. FT.
	RUDDER, WITH TABS		12·3 SQ. FT.
	RUDDER TAB		1·13 SQ. FT.

Original manufacturer's three-view drawing of the Hawker Typhoon in its earliest form with three-blade propeller. The drawing also shows both gun arrangements – 12 machine guns or four cannon. (Hawker)

This detailed twelfth-scale model was displayed in the Imperial War Museum for many years. It was made by a member of staff, C.V. McCann, in 1962.

Model of a Napier Sabre IIA engine pictured in March 1945. (Phil Butler)

RAE Farnborough photo dated 9 July 1941 showing the Typhoon's Sabre installation with the covers off. (Crown Copyright)

Groundcrew work on a Sabre engine.

which enabled the engine to be placed above the front main wing spar. This compact installation resulted in a low moment of inertia, which was why some pilots were able to report that they could 'turn inside an Fw 190', despite the Typhoon being a much larger and heavier aeroplane than the German fighter.

Fuel was carried in four self-sealing tanks in the inner wings (36 gal/164l in each leading edge tank, 41 gal/186l in each inter-spar tank) and, to avoid tail-heaviness in flight, the main tanks were used first; cigar-shaped 44 gal (200l) auxiliary drop tanks could be carried under the wings or two 90 gal (409l) long-range tanks. Early Typhoons utilised a car-door arrangement for the cockpit, but this was later replaced by a transparent sliding hood that could be jettisoned in an emergency. On the prototypes and very early production aircraft, the fairing behind the cockpit was all-metal, but from the 163rd airframe onwards this was replaced by glass panels to provide better vision, earlier aircraft being modified to the new standard.

Each wing housed two fixed forward-firing 20mm Hispano cannon with the barrels protruding well ahead of the wing leading edge, or six 0.303in Browning machine guns. Bombs or the drop tanks were carried on underwing rack fairings attached to the outer wing just outboard of the inner/outer wing joints, while rocket-projectile rails could be attached to the outer wing sections. By mid-1943 the Typhoon's equipment included two 500lb (227kg) blast-bombs, which in destructive force were equal to twice the weight of general-purpose (GP) bombs (ie, 1,000lb/454kg GP bombs).

In 1941/42 Typhoons were camouflaged in the Standard Temperate Day Fighter finish of Dark Green and Ocean Grey upper surfaces and Medium Sea Grey undersides, although a few early Mk IAs and IBs carried a Dark Green/Dark Earth scheme. The propeller spinners were usually painted Sky, the aircraft had rear fuselage bands in Sky, and from July 1942 a Yellow wing leading edge stripe appeared along with a chord-wise Yellow band across the upper wings.

During its career the Typhoon carried special identification markings because the type was frequently mistaken for the Focke-Wulf Fw 190. In November 1942 an all-White cowling was introduced, but this was too visible and was removed. Next, Black stripes on the inner wing undersides were introduced, with the space in between the Black lines now White. From D-Day, three White and two Black stripes were painted around the wings and five Black and White bands around the rear fuselage, but these later disappeared from the upper surfaces. For desert and tropical trials in 1943 EJ906 carried desert camouflage with Dark Earth and Mid-Stone upper surfaces, Azure Blue undersides and a Black spinner.

Typhoon production was in the hands of Gloster Aircraft at its Stoke Orchard factory situated to the north west of Cheltenham. Both Tornado and Typhoon prototypes and the first 15 production Typhoons came from Kingston, but all of the remaining Typhoon production (3,299 aircraft) was the responsibility of Stoke Orchard and this factory's substantial contribution to the war effort has rarely been acknowledged. No fewer than 28 RAF squadrons became major operators of the Typhoon.

Tornado

The Tornado's two-spar all-metal wings and rear fuselage were interchangeable with the Typhoon; their forward fuselages were also similar but with engine mounts suited to either the Sabre or Vulture power units. To take the Vulture motor, the Tornado's front fuselage had to be extended forward by 12in (30cm) while the wings were moved approximately 3in (8cm) lower down the fuselage sides. The most prominent difference between the two types was the Tornado's larger nose and the twin exhaust stacks on each side of the cowling rather than the Typhoon's single row, a result of the Vulture's X-24 cylinder arrangement which could not be placed over the front spar as with the Sabre. There is no evidence to confirm that any Tornados carried guns.

Data

Dimensions		
Wing span:	Tornado: Typhoon:	41ft 11in (12.78m) 41ft 7in (12.67m)
Overall length:	Tornado: Typhoon IA: Typhoon IB:	32ft 6.5in (9.92m) 31ft 10in (9.70m) 31ft 11in (9.73m)
Gross wing area:	Tornado: Typhoon:	283sq ft (26.29m²) 279sq ft (25.92m²)

Powerplant	
Tornado:	Rolls-Royce Vulture ranging from 1,760hp to 1,980hp (1,312kW to 1,476kW)
Typhoon:	2,100hp (1,566kW) Napier Sabre I, 2,180hp (1,626kW) Sabre IIA, 2,200hp (1,640kW) Sabre IIB or 2,260hp (1,685kW) Sabre IIC

Weights Fully Loaded (A&AEE Measurements)	
Tornado Vulture production:	10,600lb (4,808kg)
Typhoon Prototype P5212, 155 gal fuel:	10,620lb (4,817kg)
Typhoon IA R7617, 148 gal fuel:	10,887lb (4,938kg)
Typhoon IB DN340, 154 gal fuel + bombs:	13,248lb (6,009kg)
Typhoon IB EK497, 8 large RP:	12,426lb (5,636kg)

Armament	
Tornado Prototype and Typhoon IA:	12 x 0.303in Browning machine guns
Typhoon IB:	4 x 20mm Hispano cannon

Mk IA had no disposal weaponry. Mk IB could carry drop tanks, two 250lb (113kg), two 500lb (227kg) or two 1,000lb (454kg) bombs, two 500lb (227kg) mines, or up to 12 x 3in ground-attack rocket projectiles with 60lb (27kg) heads. A 520lb/236kg (26 segment) anti-personnel bomb was used in the final months of the war.

Tornado Performance	
P5219, 1,790hp Vulture III:	Maximum 413mph (665kph) at 22,000ft Ceiling 34,000ft
HG641, Centaurus CE.4.SM:	Maximum 430mph (692kph) at 24,000ft Service ceiling 34,500ft

Typhoon Performance	
Typhoon IA:	Maximum 405mph (652kph) at 18,000ft Service ceiling 34,000ft
Typhoon IB:	Maximum 374mph (602kph) at sea level, 412mph at height Service ceiling 35,200ft

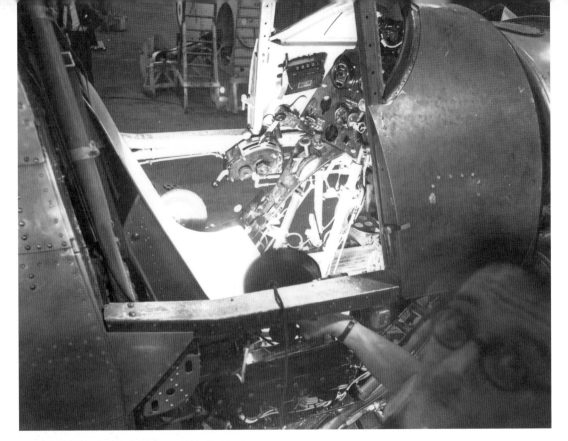

Above, left and opposite
above: Photos showing cockpit
detail for the Hawker Tornado.

Canopy and fuselage detail for the early 'car-door' type of cockpit.

Close-ups of the two forms of Typhoon cockpit canopy. Both machines appear to be presentation aircraft – the old 'car-door' version is named 'Fiji VII', the newer bubble-canopy version 'Cambay II'. Note the different exhaust arrangements. (Jet Age Museum)

Typhoon R7578 shows off the original 'closed-in' rear canopy at Gloster's Brockworth airfield.

EK288 with its 'car door' open.

Below and opposite: R7847 displays the Typhoon's layout in general and the second canopy design in particular, with a clear view now to the rear. These shots appear to have been taken at Boscombe Down.

R8809 was used for a trial installation of the sliding hood.

The value of the final bubble canopy's all-round vision is shown in this view of MN524. (Crown Copyright)

Close-up of the Typhoon's teeth on MN861 – two 20mm cannon in the wing and eight rocket projectiles on rails underneath. In fact these are linked RP (with concrete practice heads) on test at A&AEE and, except for very brief trials, were not used on operations.

This aircraft has a mix of underwing rockets and an external fuel tank.

An underwing smoke canister carried on occasion by Typhoons in trials and military exercises; this was not used on operations.

Three-quarter-rear view of R7646 again, taken at Langley.

Another view of white-nosed DN411 taken at Brockworth.

JR307 at Boscombe Down in February 1944 for trials with M10 smoke tanks. These tanks replaced those seen in close-up on page 124. (Chris Thomas)

Glossary

2 TAF	Second Tactical Air Force
A&AEE	Aircraft & Armament Experimental Establishment (Boscombe Down)
ACAS	Assistant Chief of the Air Staff
ADGB	Air Defence of Great Britain
AFDU	Air Fighting Development Unit
AA	Anti-Aircraft
ACAS(T)	Assistant Chief of the Air Staff (Technical)
AFC	Air Force Cross
ASI	Airspeed Indicated
AVM	Air Vice-Marshal
bhp	brake horsepower
Capt	Captain
Cdr	Commander
CFE	Central Fighter Establishment
CFS	Central Flying School
Cmdr	Commodore
CinC	Commander-in-Chief
CO	Commanding Officer
CofG	Centre of Gravity
CRD	Controller of Research and Development
DFC	Distinguished Flying Cross
DFM	Distinguished Flying Medal
DSC	Distinguished Service Cross
DSO	Distinguished Service Order
DTD	Director of Technical Development
FAA	Fleet Air Arm
FIU	Fighter Interception Unit
Flak	Enemy anti-aircraft gunfire, derived from Flugabwehrkanone or aircraft defence cannon
Fg Off	Flying Officer
Flt Lt	Flight Lieutenant
Flt Sgt	Flight Sergeant
FS	Fully Supercharged
GI	Ground Instruction
Gp	Group
GSU	Group Support Unit
HMS	His Majesty's Ship
Hp	Horsepower
Lt	Lieutenant
MAP	Ministry of Aircraft Production
MPA	Maximum Power Altitude

MS	Medium Supercharged
OC	Officer Commanding
OTU	Operational Training Unit
Plt Off	Pilot Officer
POW	Prisoner of War
RAAF	Royal Australian Air Force
RAE	Royal Aircraft Establishment (Farnborough)
RCAF	Royal Canadian Air Force
RN	Royal Navy
RNZAF	Royal New Zealand Air Force
RP	Rocket Projectile
rpm	Revolutions per minute
RTO	Resident Technical Officer
Sgt Plt	Sergeant Pilot
SOC	Struck Off Charge
Sqn Ldr	Squadron Leader
t/c	Thickness/chord ratio
UK	United Kingdom
USAAF	United States Army Air Force
Wg Cdr	Wing Commander

MN290 on test with Napier fitted with a (non-standard) mixed-matrix radiator. The aircraft went for trials in August 1944. (Chris Thomas)

Select Bibliography

Research for this book involved a large number of original documents in the British National Archives 'Air' and 'Avia' files, plus various private collections of photographs and documents. An unpublished 'History of Hawker Aircraft' produced by the company and its day-to-day diaries were also consulted.

Butler, Phil, 'The Hawker Tornado', *Aeromilitaria* (Winter 2009)

Bowyer, Michael J F, *Interceptor Fighters for the Royal Air Force 1939–45*, Patrick Stephens (1984)

Brown, Captain Eric 'Winkle', *Testing for Combat*, Airlife (1994)

Coles, Bob, 'Hawker Tornado', unpublished article with input from D J Campbell (1975)

Mason, Francis K, *The Hawker Typhoon and Tempest*, Aston Publications (1988)

Poulsen, C M, 'The Hawker Typhoon', *Flight*, (20 January 1944)

Price, Dr Alfred, 'The Rocket-Firing Typhoons in Normandy', *Royal Air Force Historical Society Journal 45* (2009)

Thomas, Chris, *The Hawker Typhoon*, Warpaint Series No 5 (1994)

Thomas, Chris and Shores, Christopher, *The Typhoon & Tempest Story*, Arms and Armour (1988) (The essential reference for any detailed account of the Typhoon.)